Next-Level Instructional Design

Master the four competencies shared by professional
instructional designers

Susan Nelson Spencer

BIRMINGHAM—MUMBAI

Next-Level Instructional Design

Group Product Manager: Pavan Ramchandani
Publishing Product Manager: Himani Dewan
Content Development Editor: Abhishek Jadhav
Technical Editor: Simran Udasi
Copy Editor: Safis Editing
Project Coordinator: Manthan Patel
Proofreader: Safis Editing
Indexer: Sejal DSilva
Production Designer: Aparna Bhagat
Marketing Coordinator: Nivedita Pandey

First published: April 2023

Production reference: 3030523

Published by Packt Publishing Ltd.
Livery Place
35 Livery Street
Birmingham
B3 2PB, UK.

ISBN 978-1-80181-951-0

www.packtpub.com

To my patient and empathetic husband, Ray Spencer, for his unwavering support during the writing of this book. Thank you for always understanding (and never getting angry) as I canceled engagements, worked weekends, and generally ignored my household duties. You are, and always will be, my true soulmate.

Contributors

About the author

Susan Nelson Spencer is a former fashion industry corporate trainer, college instructor, and administrator who successfully pivoted into the growing field of instructional design. Susan is the owner of Sandbox Learning Experience Design, which offers instructional design services for a wide variety of organizations, from Fortune 500 companies to non-profit foundations.

Susan holds a master of science in instructional design and technology from California State University, Fullerton, as well as post-graduate certificates in Design Thinking from IDEO, Human-Computer Interaction from Georgia Institute of Technology, and Diversity, Equity, and Inclusion from Cornell University. When she is not traveling the globe as an aspiring digital nomad, Susan lives in Southern California with her husband and two precocious standard poodles.

About the reviewers

Jo Davey is an experienced instructional designer and currently works as global head of learning for GroupM, a media company with over 48,000 employees.

She works with teams of instructional designers to lead programs as diverse as data and analytics to leadership. Her particular passion is digital learning, for which she has authored over 100 courses in her career.

Scott Onstott is a self-employed author and educator specializing in **computer-aided design (CAD)**, building information modeling, 3D modeling, and real-time visualization for architects and engineers. He has written more than a dozen books and created online courses and tutorials that have helped individuals improve their CAD, BIM, and 3D skills.

Scott is also known for his work on sacred geometry, which explores the mathematical principles underlying nature, art, and design. He has a passion for exploring consciousness, and Scott's expertise in teaching both in the classroom and online makes him a valuable resource for businesses and individuals looking to produce engaging and memorable technical courses.

Robin Wagner is a designer who's immersed in all aspects of creative technology and design. She's an instructional and learning experience designer who creates engaging instructional design assets. Her focus is on Constructivist learning theory, utilizing learner-centered design principles, UX, and LXD concepts created using a hybrid of ADDIE and SAM, along with rapid e-learning development for F2F, remote, and hybrid content.

In addition, she has been a consultant to the International Trade Centre's United Nations project on women's education in Peru, and an award-winning faculty member of the Fashion Institute of Design & Merchandising, Los Angeles.

Table of Contents

4

Creativity in Instructional Design   41

5

Project Communication in Instructional Design   63

6

The Next Level   87

Acknowledgments   91

Appendices   92

Index   101

Other Books You May Enjoy   106

Preface

The field of instructional design is a flexible, well-paying, and rewarding career. You may be reading this book as you already know people in the field and admire their work-life balance, pay, and career satisfaction. Or perhaps you've heard about this field and want to learn more. Whatever the case, welcome!

Chances are if you're a teacher, college professor, human resources professional, or even a graphic or UX designer, you may already be doing some of the work of an instructional designer without even realizing it. Reading this book will help you get to that "next level" by examining the four key competencies that are important for any aspiring instructional designer to have.

By the end of the book, you'll realize what is needed for success in the field, why these competencies are so important, and how you can better develop yours. In short, this book will help you to become a well-balanced, confident, and marketable instructional designer.

Who this book is for

This book is for those who already work in some sort of learning, coaching, visual design, or human resources capacity – and perhaps are already dabbling in instructional design. Most readers will have written some sort of learning experience in the past, whether it be in-person classes, online courses, how-to guides, PowerPoint training presentations, or even websites.

In short, if you're someone who creates learning content of *any type*, this book will teach you the best practices for moving to the next level toward becoming a true, professional instructional designer.

What this book covers

Chapter 1, *Welcome to Your New Career*, introduces the Four Competencies Model, touching upon how these competencies may relate to your current role, and how you can leverage them to pivot into a successful career in instructional design.

Chapter 2, *The Teaching Competency*, highlights the correlation between working in a teaching and/or training capacity and working in instructional design. The ADDIE model of instructional design is introduced, and the relevance of its first phase, *Analysis*, is examined as related to teaching and curriculum development.

Chapter 3, The Writing Competency, discusses the importance of writing in instructional design. Common errors in writing conventions, writing methods, and practical tips for writing in instructional design are examined. A writing assessment is offered at the end of the chapter for readers who wish to self-assess their writing skills.

Chapter 4, Creativity in Instructional Design, discusses science-based research that shows creativity *can* be nurtured. Tips for building creative thinking skills on an ongoing basis are offered. Creative problem-solving and the application of design thinking methodologies in learning design are also examined.

Chapter 5, Project Communication in Instructional Design, covers the importance of agile project management and communication throughout the ADDIE model of the instructional design process. Tips for improving communication and collaboration from an instructional designer's project's initial kick-off and managing stakeholder feedback are presented.

Chapter 6, The Next Level, wraps up The Four Competencies Model and posits the model as a way for readers to build self-efficacy in the field of instructional design. Suggestions for getting started / taking action to get to *the next level* in the field are offered.

Appendix, offers the reader the answers to writing assessments in *Chapter 3*, as well as templates to use in their own instructional design practice.

To get the most out of this book

In *Chapters 2-5*, each of the four instructional design competencies is discussed. The structure of each chapter is the same, with the hopes of respecting busy readers' time, as well as keeping the reader engaged. Each chapter covers the following:

- An explanation of what each competency in the model means as it relates to the field of instructional design

- Why it's important to build your skills in this specific area as an instructional designer

- A real-world case study highlighting the competency at play (or not at play) – and what went *right* or *wrong*

- Ways to build that specific instructional design competency, as well as further resources to dig deeper and learn more

Please note that this book is *not* about developing your software skills or learning the numerous instructional design academic theories. Instead, it's designed to help you level-up your existing core skillset and competencies quickly by offering *practical application* and *tips*.

Approach each competency chapter with self-awareness. Think about what you already know, what seems new, and how your skills match up. Even some of the most in-demand instructional designers have not mastered all four key competencies, so *leave your proverbial ego at the door and practice self-reflection* as you seek to improve your own skill set.

Keep a running list of the vocabulary you've learned, the exercises that appeal to you, the additional resources you would like to revisit when you have more time, and the template examples you might find handy in the future. *Next-Level Instructional Design* is a **practical read**, so use it in a practical way to benefit your current work situation or move toward your future aspirations.

Get in touch

Feedback from our readers is always welcome.

General feedback: If you have questions about any aspect of this book, email us at customercare@ packtpub.com and mention the book title in the subject of your message.

Errata: Although we have taken every care to ensure the accuracy of our content, mistakes do happen. If you have found a mistake in this book, we would be grateful if you would report this to us. Please visit www.packtpub.com/support/errata and fill in the form.

Piracy: If you come across any illegal copies of our works in any form on the internet, we would be grateful if you would provide us with the location address or website name. Please contact us at copyright@packt.com with a link to the material.

If you are interested in becoming an author: If there is a topic that you have expertise in and you are interested in either writing or contributing to a book, please visit authors.packtpub.com.

Share Your Thoughts

Once you've read *Next-Level Instructional Design*, we'd love to hear your thoughts! Scan the QR code below to go straight to the Amazon review page for this book and share your feedback.

https://www.amazon.in/review/create-review/error?asin=1801819513

Your review is important to us and the tech community and will help us make sure we're delivering excellent quality content.

Download a free PDF copy of this book

Thanks for purchasing this book!

Do you like to read on the go but are unable to carry your print books everywhere? Is your eBook purchase not compatible with the device of your choice?

Don't worry, now with every Packt book you get a DRM-free PDF version of that book at no cost.

Read anywhere, any place, on any device. Search, copy, and paste code from your favorite technical books directly into your application.

The perks don't stop there, you can get exclusive access to discounts, newsletters, and great free content in your inbox daily

Follow these simple steps to get the benefits:

1. Scan the QR code or visit the link below

https://packt.link/free-ebook/9781801819510

2. Submit your proof of purchase
3. That's it! We'll send your free PDF and other benefits to your email directly

1

Welcome to Your New Career

If you're reading this book about becoming a successful instructional designer, the chances are you're looking for a bit of career enhancement or even a career change. You may be reading it because you don't have the time or money to invest in further formalized education in instructional design, or perhaps because you're being asked to complete learning projects at work and are looking for more direction.

Whatever your circumstance, congratulations on taking a significant first step by reading this book!

If you teach or train others in a classroom setting, either in-person or virtually, you've already done some of the work an **Instructional Designer** (**ID**) does. Likewise, if you design materials, such as how-to guides, PowerPoint presentations, or even websites, you're already doing some of the work of an instructional designer.

You're most likely someone who's often called upon to help others learn in your current role. Generally speaking, if you help others to learn, you probably enjoy learning as well.

An in-demand field

The field of instructional design has burgeoned over the past few years. Due to factors beyond our control, such as the global pandemic and the ensuing move toward more virtual versus in-person instruction, the demand for online learning has dramatically increased. Companies and educational institutions have realized that yes, people can learn online, and that it's often a far lower-cost alternative to in-person training.

Hence, the demand for "IDs", as the role is often referred to, has grown exponentially (`https://bit.ly/3YEwKRK`). Instructional design is a field that's projected to grow at a rate of eight percent or more annually (`http://bit.ly/3xl1RFT`).

Moreover, working as an ID earns high marks for work-life balance, job satisfaction, low stress, pay, and an overall perceived benefit to society (`http://bit.ly/3lHILqA`).

There's no great mystery here: for the right person, being an instructional designer is a rewarding and lucrative career path. You might be wondering, *What does an ID actually do?* Even though you'll read many real-world cases about instructional design in this book, let's start with a top-level view.

Functions of an instructional designer

On a day-to-day basis as an ID, you're most likely to do the following:

- Work with stakeholders to ensure the learning experience you're charged with creating meets its desired learning objectives, and is developed in the best possible learning mode for the target audience

- Learn about new topics, trends, and industries by working with subject matter experts and other stakeholders

- Research on your own to further structure learning content

- Analyze the content you've received and developed to structure it in a way that will be appropriate for your target audience

- Write instructional content on the topics you've just learned about

- Use learning-specific software tools that allow you to translate written content into an engaging virtual learning course

- Transform your written content into engaging e-learning interactions and creative graphical representations

- Incorporate feedback that you receive through each phase of course development to satisfy all stakeholders and ensure the *learning experience* is accurate, meets its learning objectives, and is engaging

Now that you've realized it's quite possible you're already doing the work of an instructional designer. It's time to look through the unique lens this book will offer you into the field of instructional design. It's called **The Four Competencies Model**.

Placing yourself within The Four Competencies Model

The Four Competencies Model you will find throughout this book is not a scientific model, but instead is based on my experience in higher education, not-for-profit, and corporate instructional design. The model follows my empirical observations from working with or observing the skills of the most successful IDs.

What I've observed is that successful IDs possess some degree of strength in all four competency areas - and believe it or not, none of these areas have to do with software development skills.

The four key competencies that the most successful IDs possess have to do with their ability to teach, write, create, and collaborate successfully with others:

I can... TEACH	I can... WRITE
I can... CREATE	I can... COMMUNICATE

Figure 1.1 – The Four Competencies Model

It's a bit of *back to basics*, isn't it? However, it is these four *core* competencies that are often missing in instructional design work!

It's my hope that by developing an awareness of these four competency areas, you will be able to:

- Identify your current skills and strengths
- Apply them toward a career in instructional design
- Realize which areas you might need to build
- Develop your weaker competencies so that you become a well-rounded ID who is capable of taking on all sorts of assignments

It sounds like a tall order, doesn't it? Here's the good news: not all people have the same level of skill in each competency. In fact, it's quite rare for someone to be expertly gifted in each. As such, the goal of this book is to offer you practical tips on how to further build your skills in each competency area.

Each of the four competencies has been given a separate chapter. As you move through the content, make time to do some self-reflection.

Ask yourself:

- Have I been asked to do this type of work before, albeit in a different environment or context?
- Is this a competency or skill that I excel in, am adequate at, or perhaps need to build?
- Which of the practical tips offered in each chapter will allow me to build upon this competency?

"Now we have the introduction part out of the way, You're now ready to get started on your new career! We'll start with the first piece of The Four Competencies framework: examining your **Teaching Competency**."

2

The Teaching Competency

"Good teaching is instructional design. Your lesson planning, ability to meet standards, and passion are directly responsible for your success in teaching. It's no different as an instructional designer, except now it's learning objectives, design, and development."

– *Alex Phung, former middle-school math teacher turned instructional designer*

The first, and perhaps the most important, element of The Four Competencies Model is your ability to *think like an educator*. By understanding how to analyze and structure content as an educator does, you'll be able to help people learn better from the courses you design.

I can... **TEACH**	I can... *WRITE*
I can... *CREATE*	I can... *COMMUNICATE*

Figure 2.1 – The Teaching Competency

In this chapter, you will learn about:

- The similarities between teaching, curriculum design, and instructional design

- How knowing learning theories, structuring content, and learning objectives will help you as an ID

- The **ADDIE model** of instructional design, specifically the *analysis* phase which correlates most closely to teaching and training

- The importance of the *analysis* phase and knowing your target audience

- How to build your teaching competency skills as an ID

How does being a good instructor relate to being an effective ID?

As a current or former teacher, college instructor, or even corporate trainer, you have a strong start on transitioning into instructional design. This is because:

- You know what a *learning objective* (*LO*) is and have probably written many
- You understand the importance of *knowing your learner*
- You've already *designed curricula* and lesson plans
- You've *written assessments* (quizzes and exams)
- You've perhaps *studied learning theories* and how people learn best
- You're *familiar with different instructional methods* and how to engage learners by applying these concepts to practical applications

These are all aspects of instructional design. In fact, already knowing these basics of learning gives you a leg-up in the field of instructional design – especially in the early phases of the ID process.

These early activities in an instructional design project represent the gathering and structuring of content. Needless to say, the stages of content gathering and analysis are the backbone of any successful learning experience.

In fact, other terms used for the role of an instructional designer include **learning designer** and **learning experience designer**. If you're a teacher or trainer of any kind, you've probably gathered and analyzed content loads of times!

What if I've "only" trained others in a non-educational setting?

If you've not been in an educational setting but have taught others via writing corporate training curricula, you have many of the same teaching competency skills under your belt. **Training is teaching, and instructional design is all about training others**.

Inevitably, you've had to tell your learners what they'll be learning in a given seminar or PowerPoint presentation, structure the material logically, present it in a visually engaging fashion, and perhaps offer some sort of assessment of learning.

In short, you have teaching competency as well, just in a different context. You might not have studied the learning theories or instructional methods that a K-12 teacher has, but you inherently know what works for your organization's learners and how to train them effectively.

What if I've been a technical writer/editor but haven't formally taught?

If this is you, admittedly your stronger competencies might fall into one of the other three competencies (such as writing). Being a strong writer is the backbone of instructional design. However, remember: if you're an effective non-fiction writer, you're also in some way *instructing* others.

Strong non-fiction, technically oriented writers and editors know how to analyze and structure content for learning purposes. While you might not be familiar with the preceding learning theories or instructional methods or even have never 'presented' your content, as a technical writer, you're still writing toward an end goal of learning.

The bottom line is that on some level, you might have also taught through *written communication*. The practical tips and sources offered at the end of this chapter will help you to quickly level-up your knowledge of learning theories and instructional methods and direct your strong writing skills toward an instructional perspective.

What if I've "only" been a visual/graphic or UX/UI designer?

In this case, you have the unique advantage of having taught others primarily through visual representation. Graphic and UX/UI design is all about visual communications. If you're able to adeptly create something that is visually pleasing and engaging to a target audience, you are already skilled at reaching your target audience.

While the teaching competency might not be your strong suit (or perhaps never even considered), you will immediately have advantages in the *creating* and *collaboration* competencies, as you are familiar with the basics of visual design and, most likely, possess excellent creative software development skills.

Moreover, you're used to constant input from others in your work. Unless you have also taught graphic or UX/UI design, you'll most likely need to assume that the teaching (and writing) competencies are areas for which you will need to develop.

Teaching and training as related to instructional design

In thinking about your own experience, reflect upon about the teachers, college instructors, or trainers you've had over your lifetime: which were the most effective? Which was the most influential on your life and motivated you to move in new directions?

In my own experience as a college instructor and administrator for over 20 years, I have found that both classroom and online instructors are most successful when they:

- Are adaptable
- Understand their learners and the differences in the classroom
- Have strong and precise written and verbal communication skills
- Are patient and empathetic
- Structure and deliver content in a way that all learners understand
- Are enthusiastic and set a positive tone
- Are consistent and fair-minded in assessment and grading practices
- Are available and supportive toward getting others to learn

Let's focus on the online piece of teaching, and take a look at what makes an effective *online* instructor, as much of instructional design involves designing learning that will be delivered as online, for example eLearning. Research has shown that some of the key success factors for instructors teaching in an independent, eLearning environment include *setting learner expectations early, incorporating readily available materials, providing a course-closing activity, and asking for feedback* (`https://elearningindustry.com/10-best-practices-effective-online-teacher`). **These are also aspects of a well-designed learning experience in the field of instructional design**.

Similarities between teaching and instructional design

In reviewing my experiential list of *what it takes to be an effective instructor*, we can see many correlations between instructional designers and effective online and classroom teachers.

An effective instructional designer must have a strong command of written communication and possess the ability to verbally present and defend their ideas backed by readily available resources. They need to lay out and structure learner expectations from the outset. So does an effective teacher or trainer.

Moreover, empathy and patience are key tenets of the most successful instructional designers. IDs need to be able to put themselves into the learner's shoes, as they create courses and patiently wait for stakeholder feedback. Lastly, a good ID wants to help others to learn and needs to be fair-minded when it comes to **Subject Matter Expert (SME)**, stakeholder, and learner feedback, and even when creating assessments.

From these similarities, I'd like to dive a bit deeper and offer you some further insights into the importance of *teaching as an instructional designer* and the interconnectedness of having been an effective instructor and becoming an effective instructional designer. We'll call this the *takeaways* section.

Takeaway 1 – Teaching is designing curricula. Instructional design is, too.

Curriculum design is a bit of its own art form; anyone who's ever been charged with structuring their own course, class, or lesson plan can attest to this. It's a process that needs to consider the learning environment, the learner, and the content at hand. The basic aspects of curriculum design include the following:

- Knowing who your learner is and what they might already know (or not know)
- Understanding what your learner aims to get out of the learning experience
- Identifying your course, class, or lesson's **learning objectives** (**LOs**) and goals
- Making the connection between how your learning experience will allow your learners to attain the course LOs
- Analyzing the best/most logical sequence and structure of the material to attain the LOs you've set forth
- Deciding what kind of activities you'll develop to interest and engage the learner

- Planning for how you'll check their knowledge before, during, and at the end of the learning experience to gauge for learning needed, and later attained

- Identifying how you'll follow up to see whether the learning is truly realized

- Developing the types of feedback questions that you'll ask for to consistently iterate and improve the quality of your course, class, or lesson

Now, let's compare these concepts to the basic aspects of instructional design by using one of the most important instructional design process frameworks, **ADDIE** which stands for *Analysis, Design, Development, Implementation, and Evaluation*. ADDIE was first developed for military training purposes at Florida State University in 1975. Due to its simplicity, ADDIE has now been adopted by thousands of instructional designers delivering a wide range of training and educational content. While there are other frameworks for the instructional design process, such as the **Successive Approximation Model (SAM)** – as discussed later in this book – the ADDIE model is a great place to start for those who are newer to instructional design.

> Glossary
> **ADDIE** stands for **analysis, design, development, implementation, and evaluation**.

Figure 2.2 – Dave Braunschweig under a CC-BY-SA-3.0 license

The first phase of the ADDIE model, *Analysis*, is probably the most important phase of the instructional design process, and certainly the most closely related to teaching and curriculum development. The good news for those with any type of instructional background is that you've probably done this type of analysis for courses, classes, or lessons you've written time and time again – without ever realizing it.

The analysis phase is where you will learn more about your audience, their needs, and the solution you'll provide to them. Think of this as a needs assessment of sorts: you need to figure out *if the training will be a solution to the problem/knowledge gap at hand*. If the learning gap exists because of other organizational culture issues, then no amount of training will help. This is what your needs assessment should uncover.

In the analysis phase, you'll also be taking a long look at your target learner audience: after all, you need to know who you're designing this training for! You need to know about their prior learning efforts, level of subject knowledge, learning mode preferences, motivation to complete the training, and learning style. You'll also need to uncover any other barriers to learning, such as English as a second language, or specific technical or software limitations.

Lastly, after you've gleaned whether the training will indeed be a solution to a learning gap and who the learner is, you'll need to figure out how you can map the training experience's proposed LOs to *tangible organizational performance goals*. This is especially important if you're designing learning in a corporate environment, versus for an educational institution.

As you can see, the *analysis* phase of ADDIE is an important step for all learning experiences, but is often not completed thoroughly. Stakeholders will ask their instructional design team to move straight to the *Design* phase of ADDIE, without the proposed audience's needs - or the learning solutions that should be provided to them.

Now, let's look at how the ability to design curricula maps to the instructional design ADDIE process:

Teaching/curriculum design	->	Instructional design/ADDIE analysis phase
• Who your target learner is, and what they might already know (or not know)	->	• Completing a target learner analysis to fully identify and understand your learner
• What they aim to get out of the learning experience • What your course, class, or lesson's LOs are	->	• Conducting a learning needs assessment
• How you'll attain your LOs for the lesson • How you can best logically sequence/structure the material to attain the LOs you've set forth	->	• Mapping your LOs to future tangible performance

Takeaway 2 – Teaching is helping others to learn. So is instructional design

If you've wondered why you've often landed in some sort of teaching or training capacity, it's probably because you enjoy helping others. On some level, you're probably patient, empathetic, and/or even altruistic. It's no wonder why so many people correlate teaching to volunteerism (not just because of the pay!): there's hard neuroscience behind feeling good after you've helped someone.

It's called the *Helper's High*. After doing a good act or helping someone, it's been found that our bodies release endorphins, which help to lift mood. In fact, according to a national survey done by the US-based UnitedHealth Group, 94 percent of people who volunteered/helped others in the last

12 months said that it improved their mood (`https://projecthelping.org/benefits-of-volunteering/`).

It's been found that helping others also increases gratitude, increases life satisfaction, distracts you from your own problems, and even has been found to improve physical health (`https://www.huffpost.com/entry/benefits-of-volunteering_b_4151540`).

Will you see the lightbulb turn on for your students and get that *helping high* in instructional design? Probably not quite in the same way. But you *will* work alongside others to garner feedback about learning experiences you've designed, and hopefully, hear some reviews from learners and stakeholders first-hand.

> **Think about it**
>
> Many IDs I know often get the same helping high from simply *knowing* that we are designing learning in key subject areas that will help others to grow and learn. The feeling may not be as "direct" as in teaching, but it's the same long-term feel-good outcome.

Takeaway 3 – Instructors enjoy learning new things, so do instructional designers

Another reason why you might be in some sort of sort of teaching or training capacity is that you enjoy learning. Good teachers are always learning something new to help their students, as are good instructional designers. Quite honestly, instructional design is a field full of learning nerds who not only enjoy imparting knowledge to others, but "learning a little about a lot" themselves.

And why not continue to learn? Not only does it foster a growth mindset, but research has also shown that level of education is the single most telling factor in higher levels of health and living longer. People who are more deeply engaged in continuous learning have also been found to have higher levels of happiness and overall well-being (`https://bit.ly/3XsxlEF`).

> **Pause and reflect**
>
> No matter what you've done before, if you're open, curious, and enjoy researching new topics, the Teaching Competency in instructional design will come naturally to you.

Use cases

Consider this the practical case study section of each of our four competency chapters. In this first case study, we'll look at the *Teaching Competency* through the lens of the instructional design model ADDIE and the analysis phase. Then, in the next case, we'll pivot to learning and instructional science.

In both cases, you'll be able to see where the skills of someone who has taught and trained others are directly related to instructional design.

Use case 1 – your target learner audience *is* important

I was working as the contract instructional designer for a nonprofit organization, whose mission is to "bring leadership learning to every stage of life, from Pre-K to adulthood". I was brought on to create leadership learning experiences for their adult learning division, so that narrowed the target audience down a bit.

In my initial interviews and scoping sessions with the stakeholders of this small, nonprofit organization, it dawned on me that all three stakeholders had different ideas about who their target learner was and how learning should be delivered.

The first stakeholder advocated for the target learner as *all millennials*, mostly male, in U.S. corporate jobs – for whom the courses I would be developing would be sold on a *public-facing website*.

> **Pause and reflect:**
>
> Is this target definition realistic given the following fact?
>
> **The number of male millennials (aged 25–44) in the U.S. as of 2022 is 45 million** (`https://www.marketingcharts.com/featured-30401`).
>
> A **target audience** (`https://www.digitalmarketing.org/blog/what-is-target-audience`) is a group of people defined based on their common characteristics, such as demographics and behaviors. This could be gender, age, location, purchasing power, profession, income, marital status, and more.

In instructional design, you need to think about your target market in terms of training and **desired behavior change**. In your initial needs assessment, you'll want to establish the following:

- The level of your learner's expertise and role – for example, are they beginners, experts, executives, or technicians?

- The geographical location of your learners – for example, being sensitive to English-as-a-second language learners, and the use of country-specific euphemisms or slang

- The type of work they do – for example, are they new employees? Do they do manual labor, do they have a desk job, or is this a *train-the-trainer* learning group?

The second stakeholder was pushing for "not limiting our learning to just the public", and for "selling our leadership courses to corporate clients". This stakeholder had the same age range in mind as the first but gave more details, such as "Male millennials who usually live in the middle of the U.S. are mid-level managers and watch sports". He recommended creating the same courses for public consumption as for corporate learners.

The third stakeholder recommended creating *two sets of courses*: one for the public-facing website, and one for corporate-only clients. They had the same general description of their learner as stakeholder two, except they recommended differentiating the learning modalities: asynchronous eLearning for the public who would be purchasing on their website and synchronous, and cohort-based eLearning for corporate clients, meaning that these learners would learn together as a group.

> **Think about it**
>
> Knowing what you now know at this point of the story and chapter, what would you have done as the newly-hired contract ID on this project?
>
> A. Politely tell them that you could not take on the project since they had not yet identified a true target learner.
>
> B. Try to help them to fine-tune their target audience down, A LOT.
>
> C. Nothing; the more learners identified, the merrier.
>
> D. RUN!

I ended up staying on the project and choosing option *B*. I recommended that they hire a marketing firm to narrow down their learner target market and figure out how to brand and sell their products.

- Narrow down their learner focus.
- Figure out how to brand and sell their learning products.

Despite hiring a market research firm, my learning design and development were moving faster than the marketing firm's target market segmentation efforts, so their research never did help to further define my target audience past a potential 45 million learners!

> **Takeaway**
>
> Creating a course without knowing your audience is like shooting in the dark and hoping you'll hit the target.

In the end, the lack of target market focus culminated with a *free test run* of my developed course version with a group of poorly-chosen, mid-level managers from three very different organizations: an urban not-for-profit community activist organization, a group of males from a competitive organization in the membership leadership space, and Generation Z college students/recent graduates from the founder of the nonprofit organization's college alma mater (for which he was a large donor).

> **Think about it**
>
> These selected test learners had no stake or motivation to complete the course. They were taking it for free and were accountable to nobody. They also had little in common as cohorts. We can all guess how this played out!

At the end of our 10-week beta course trial run, only 10% of this target cohort completed the course. I was mortified: my beautiful and engaging course only had a 10% completion rate. I truly felt like an abject failure (especially as this was my first contract ID role), and soon after left the project.

I learned that the client later created *two versions* of the course I designed and developed to segment their target learner further. A step in the right direction, but I also learned that the courses they rolled out were almost identical!

> ### Takeaway
> Adult learners fully engage in learning *only* if it is relevant to their needs and helps them solve their immediate problems.

In retrospect, this was my first direct contract as an instructional designer. I made many mistakes, starting with *accepting an instructional design project for an ambiguous target market*. With more experience, I would have insisted on the nonprofit conducting a proper analysis of their learner audience *before* accepting the project. As it stood, I really didn't know any of the following:

- Who I was designing the training for
- Anything at all about the learner's prior learning efforts
- The learner's level of subject knowledge in leadership (or if they were even leaders)
- The learner's modality preferences
- Their motivation to complete the training
- Their learning style
- Any other barriers to learning (such as English as a second language, software limitations, and more)

I didn't really know anything specific about my learner!

I think if I had more experience in the *analysis* phase of ADDIE and had put some of my previous teaching/curriculum design skills into place, I would have dug much deeper into this organization's idea of a target market and how they wanted to deliver their learning.

Use case 2 – the importance of well-structured content

The **hierarchy of information** presented, or how information is *structured*, is just as important in instructional design as it is in teaching. Think about it: we wouldn't try to teach a child division before multiplication, or multiplication before addition, would we? The same sort of information hierarchy holds true with instructional design. In fact, some higher-level ID jobs are even called **learning architects**.

This use case is about a project that I inherited as a *Do-over*, or revision project. The client, a large digital media agency, requested that I review a course that had been assigned recently – which she thought was confusing to the learner as it stood. It was designed as a self-paced eLearning course for new employees just joining the agency. The client wanted to keep the eLearning delivery mode, as she could reach more learners at once with self-paced eLearning.

The course topic was an overview of what a new employee to the agency would need to know on day 1 of their job – a technical lay of the land of sorts. The learner would need to be able to understand different types of digital advertising placement, how and where they are used, and the work roles responsible for specific tasks when working with clients.

The course was designed in a learning software/course authoring tool called Articulate Rise 360™, an ID-friendly tool that allows the user to create a variety of predetermined images, text, and learner interaction activities by selecting different learning blocks to design the content.

One of the great advantages of having trained or taught others is that you know you need to teach your learners how to walk before they run. You also know that you can't overload the learner with too much information at once, and that information is best presented in small, related chunks.

Breaking down information in this way is especially important when creating self-paced eLearning courses, like the course we're discussing. Since the learner is on their own to make sense of what is being presented to them, content needs to be organized in a progressive, logical way for chunking.

Moreover, the content needs to be presented in groups of related information. Related groups or chunks of information are always more meaningful than random bits of content!

> **Pause and reflect**
> If you've taught before, does the concept of *chunking* small groups of related information sound familiar? If so, think of an example of how you used this instructional approach in the past – and a current project for which you can apply chunking to now.

I soon realized that the concept of breaking down large pieces of information into smaller ones had not been followed in this course. It was apparent that:

- **The LOs had not been well thought-out and didn't reflect the scope of the content**. The key skills that the new employee would need to perform were not adequately represented in the course's LOs.

- As a result, **the content did not follow a logical progression** (from foundational concepts to more complicated ones).

- **The course content was over-chunked**. There were standalone concepts that needed to be connected to their parent concepts. Any learner, especially a brand-new employee, would have had a difficult time connecting these random bits of information.

I ended up dissecting the content and restructuring the course. I went back through and grouped together large groups of conceptually related content. I created *course modules* to reflect these larger groups of related content.

Then, I chunked these large groups of content further down into *lessons*, and from there, I created specific **color and text hierarchy signposts** at the *screen level* to notify the learner that they were moving from one topic or subtopic to another.

In the following example, you can see that I've used navy blue as the color background signpost, showing a relationship between one subtopic and another. The teal color is used as a signpost to inform the learner that they are moving to the next subtopic:

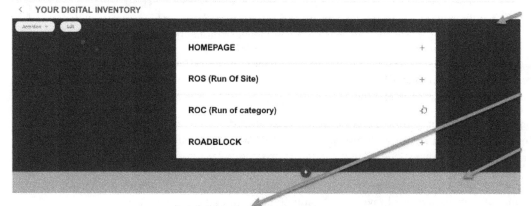

Figure 2.3 – Color and text signposts

> **Think about it**
>
> Creating an old-fashioned course outline never goes out of style. Don't fall into the trap of jumping right into design and development without first analyzing and chunking your content to create a logical information hierarchy.

I hope the above case studies help you put the concept of *thinking like an educator* in instructional design into context. Talk about live and learn! We'll now move onto the final section of this chapter, which is designed to help you **build your Teaching Competency** skills.

Build your teaching competency

You've completed an important first step toward your new career by reading this chapter. I hope that *The Four Competencies Model*, and the first aspect of it has opened your eyes to the many similarities between the skills of an effective teacher, trainer, college instructor, writer, and visual designer and those of an instructional designer.

Now, it's time to deliver upon a few resources that I believe will help you to hone your *Teaching Competency*. Consider this a cafeteria-style offering: take what you want, leave what you don't.

Build your needs assessment skills

The first step in developing any type of training should always be a needs assessment with your stakeholders. Often, stakeholders will think they know exactly what their organizational performance problems are, but as the instructional designer, you'll want to *verify* what people are currently doing. Additionally, you'll want to assess what the performance gap is between the *actual* and your stakeholder's *desired* performance level. If you can, it's even helpful to learn *why* people aren't performing to the level that your stakeholders desire.

Down the road, skipping this step can lead to developing a course with the wrong amount of content, or even *incorrect or irrelevant* training content, for the target learner.

As such, I've curated a few articles here for you that explain why conducting a needs assessment is important, and how to go about doing one:

- **eLearning Industry**: `https://elearningindustry.com/the-what-why-and-how-of-needs-assessments`
- **The eLearning Designer's Academy by Tim Slade**: `https://www.youtube.com/watch?v=TDZ6_iVZlt0`
- **Learning Solutions Magazine**: `https://learningsolutionsmag.com/articles/instructional-design-begins-with-needs-assessment`

Build your skills in defining a target learner audience

As mentioned in *Use Case 1* earlier in the chapter, defining your target audience is an important early step in the instructional design process. Without knowing the basics of who your target learner really is, you run the risk of building a course that is entirely off-kilter for your learner – and not hitting your LOs/performance goals. For my former teachers, think of this as being told you're teaching fourth graders, but really, your learners are seventh graders! Or just think of the *45 million* male millennials I was asked to capture in my first project as a contract ID!

It's important to learn how to ask the right questions of your clients and/or stakeholders. Here are a few resources to help you get started with your target learner analysis:

- **Shift**: `https://www.shiftelearning.com/blog/template-elearning-audience-analysis`

- **e-LearningHeroes**: `https://community.articulate.com/articles/how-to-do-an-e-learning-audience-analysis`

- **eLearning Industry**: `https://elearningindustry.com/how-use-audience-analysis-and-learner-personas`

Build your learning objective (LO) writing skills with Bloom's Taxonomy

We've discussed the development of LOs as an important beginning step in an instructional design project. As with much of the other content in this chapter, developing LO's belongs squarely in the ADDIE *analysis* phase.

Think of your LOs as the foundation for everything you design later in the course – and the basis for which you can measure actual behavior change after the course has been completed by your target learners.

Believe it or not, writing measurable LOs is a bit of an art form, and IDs love to geek out over LO development. Often, you can tell who's a more experienced ID from a less experienced one through their use of Bloom's taxonomy (`https://cft.vanderbilt.edu/guides-sub-pages/blooms-taxonomy/`).

Bloom's (as IDs affectionately refer to it) is the cornerstone for choosing the correct *verb* as related to the level of learning you want your target audience to complete.

In use with teachers, college instructors, and instructional designers for over 50 years, Bloom's taxonomy lays out six levels of learning. In 2001, a group of educators and cognitive psychologists revised Bloom's in their text, *A Taxonomy for Teaching, Learning, and Assessment* (`https://bit.ly/3YTSEQo`), in which they redefined six levels of learning, from basic recall to creation, and added dynamic *action* verbs describing the cognitive processes people use when acquiring knowledge, as shown in the following revised Bloom's taxonomy model:

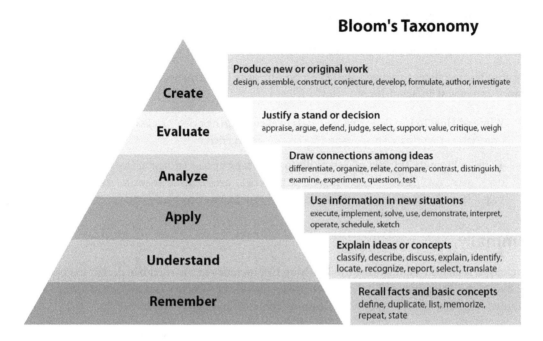

Bloom's Taxonomy

Create — Produce new or original work
design, assemble, construct, conjecture, develop, formulate, author, investigate

Evaluate — Justify a stand or decision
appraise, argue, defend, judge, select, support, value, critique, weigh

Analyze — Draw connections among ideas
differentiate, organize, relate, compare, contrast, distinguish, examine, experiment, question, test

Apply — Use information in new situations
execute, implement, solve, use, demonstrate, interpret, operate, schedule, sketch

Understand — Explain ideas or concepts
classify, describe, discuss, explain, identify, locate, recognize, report, select, translate

Remember — Recall facts and basic concepts
define, duplicate, list, memorize, repeat, state

Figure 2.4 – Bloom's taxonomy , Armstrong, P. (2010). Bloom's Taxonomy. Vanderbilt University Center for Teaching, (https://cft.vanderbilt.edu/guides-sub-pages/blooms-taxonomy/)

Here are some resources that will help you build your skills in writing LOs. You'll note that each resource listed cites *Bloom's taxonomy*:

- **How to Write Learning Objectives with Blooms Taxonomy**: `https://www.youtube.com/watch?v=QXGOjzcQdhQ`

- **Bloom's Taxonomy**: `https://cft.vanderbilt.edu/guides-sub-pages/blooms-taxonomy/`

- **An Introduction to Bloom's Taxonomy for Instructional Designers**: `https://community.articulate.com/series/practical-instructional-design-how-tos/articles/blooms-taxonomy-elearning-instructional-design`

Build your skills in setting performance goals

LOs and performance goals are, indeed, similar. However, one of the key differences is that performance goals are used to improve job performance (I'm talking to you, corporate IDs!).

That said, when your stakeholders are skeptical of **what someone will really take away** from your learning, discuss setting performance goals to measure **before and after** the training behaviors.

Developing specific and actionable performance goals is another art form in itself, as you'll need to work closely with your stakeholders to clearly define the desired behavior change (the new skills acquired) and how this new performance level can be observed and measured.

Here are a few resources to get you started on how to write performance goals in order to measure behavior and new skills acquisition:

- **Why and How To Use Performance Goals in eLearning**: `https://elearningindustry.com/use-performance-goals-in-elearning`
- **4 Tips to Promote Transfer of New Skills to the Job**: `https://community.articulate.com/series/practical-instructional-design-how-tos/articles/4-tips-to-promote-transfer-of-new-skills-to-the-job`

Summary

Hopefully, this chapter highlighting the **Teaching Competency** in instructional design has opened your eyes to the similarities and differences between the role of a teacher, trainer, or instructor - and anyone who has created written or visual learning content - and that of an ID.

Parlaying teaching skills into instructional design is, in my opinion, one of the best things a new ID can do for their career. These early analysis activities in an instructional design project represent the gathering and structuring of content and become the backbone of any successful learning experience.

If you haven't had any experience in teaching or training, my hope is that this chapter has assisted you in developing and strengthening your ID **teaching competency**. The content and resources in the chapter are designed to help someone understand foundational instructional competencies.

Even if you've never heard of anything that's been discussed in this chapter before, you'll now have the knowledge to think like an educator when starting your next instructional design project. You're off to a solid start!

In the next chapter, we'll shift to the second ID competency in our model: **The Writing Competency**.

The Writing Competency

"When instructional writing is done well, it has the power to reduce cognitive load, increase memory retention, and increase content engagement. It's a catalyst for learning, not a blocker."

– Andrew Debell, author and instructional designer

Strong writing skills are important in instructional design. I spend at least 50% of my time on each ID project outlining, structuring, and revising my writing – and that doesn't include time spent on client-requested revisions. In fact, some sources cite that writing comprises 80% of the average time spent on an instructional design project (`https://tinyurl.com/yunbrthk`). That's huge!

I can...	I can...
TEACH	<u>WRITE</u>
I can...	I can...
CREATE	*COMMUNICATE*

Figure 3.1 – The Four Competencies Model

In this chapter, we'll review:

- What writing for ID means and how to do it

- A case study that highlights some common writing-for-ID pitfalls

- Some practical tips and additional resources you can reference to build your writing competency

Writing may or may not come easily to you. You may love it or loathe it. But here's the newsflash: You must be at least a *competent* writer to excel in ID. Even if you're an ace at Articulate Storyline development, if the underlying structure of your online course is poorly structured, rife with grammatical errors, or doesn't engage the learner, your courses will be ineffective.

As an instructional designer, it's the learning experiences you develop that organizations rely on to change behavior, so writing clearly and persuasively is important.

I've worked for, with, and even hired fellow instructional designers who can and cannot write well. On each project, writing mattered. In fact, projects were often slowed due to poor content structuring/ writing skills or the inability to capture the client's *voice*.

> **Glossary**
> **Voice** in writing for instructional design is often dictated by a company's writing/brand style guide. It refers to how punctuation, syntax, point of view (person), tone, and choice of words are used.

In my opinion, your writing competency is even more important than being a strong course developer. As an ID professional, you can always outsource an ID developer, but it's much more difficult to outsource an effective course writer that understands all the nuances of an organization's writing style and their needs for the course you're designing.

What is writing for ID?

One of the challenges (and joys!) of being an instructional designer is that you get to learn about a variety of professions and subjects all the time. I've written and designed courses for everything from patent law in candy-making to digital marketing 101, to how to take care of yourself.

Given the wide range of topics your work may lead you to, you may be asked to write in a variety of styles. Often, how you approach your writing style is dependent upon the company/client and subject matter, but there are some common threads that run throughout all ID projects.

The most important takeaway here is that **writing for instructional design needs to motivate the learner**. In addition to conveying the content through designed interactions in whichever course authoring software tool you're using, your learner needs to learn.

As instructional designers, we're hired to change people's behaviors, so our work needs to be engaging and clear enough to deliver these behavior-changing concepts. Inevitably, how we write the course is the backbone for this.

As instructional designers, we need to be able to do the following:

- **Structure and organize course content clearly** - eliminate random, unassociated bits of content
- **Be concise** - avoid redundant wording and sentence structure
- **Watch for common grammatical and punctuation errors** - always scan for typos
- **Be engaging and motivating** - through writing in a conversational tone

Let's take a closer look at each of these points.

Structuring your course content clearly

Disorganized content confuses learners. While this might seem like a completely basic concept, as an ID, it's easy to get excited about your project and dive right into its design phase before properly structuring your content.

In the preceding chapter, we discussed the importance of conducting a needs assessment and target audience analysis, or answering the questions of *Why?*, *Who?*, and *What's* the end goal? Now, we need to tie back to those **learning objectives (LOs)** we wrote and properly structure our content.

Knowing your higher and lower-order concerns

Higher-order and **lower-order concerns** are English professor-type terms that refer to structuring the big picture (higher-order) and related content (lower-order) of your course content. Before diving into an authoring tool to design and develop, I like to sit down and create a content map that outlines the *higher-order* structure of the course using the LOs I've developed.

I tend to do this even if the client has not asked for a formal outline or design document, as I like to organize my thoughts visually. For me, this involves a simple Google doc drawing that highlights what I see as the overall structure of the course. Unless I'm designing a **microlearning**, I usually tie each lesson to a learning objective, then create topics and sub-topics from there.

> Glossary
>
> **Microlearning** refers to chunking an eLearning course into several bite-size learning elements, often delivered via mobile-capable technology. The idea is that shorter micro-courses will prevent the learner from zoning out or disengaging from the course content and provide 'quick hits' of key information to the learner. Often, a microlearning course may relate to just one learning objective.

Contrary to popular belief, it's not necessary to get too granular or complete a complicated flowchart to get your course's basic structure down – plus, your stakeholders will appreciate the simplicity of your map.

Here's an example of a content map for a 30-minute Articulate Rise™ course I developed:

Managing Yourself Course Outline

Content Map

Figure 3.2 – Higher-order course content map for the "Managing Yourself" course

From there, depending on the length of the course, I'll create a **design document** following the content map that's split into called-out sections for each lesson. Here, I will outline the initial draft content first, take a bit of a break, then return to the design document to add my ideas surrounding visuals, job aids, learner activities, and interactions.

In the end, I will make sure to write the initial draft content as close as it will appear on screen in the online course for my stakeholders to review.

> **Glossary**
> A **design document** is the blueprint for a course. It shows the overall course structure and detailed information for each course module or lesson.

The following example is a design document for the same course, using the course authoring software tool Articulate Rise 360™. Here, we see the progression of higher- to lower-order concerns: an introduction to a new topic (*Procrastination*) within the *Time Management* lesson is called out in the content map.

Here's the design document for the same 30-minute Articulate Rise™ course:

[TXT + HDG]	**PROCRASTINATION** Almost everyone procrastinates to some degree. In fact, according to a recent study, 88% of the workforce admits that they prograstinate at least one hour a day. It's a giant problem! Obviously the benefits to not procrastinating include getting more done and higher productivity. But do you know there're additional benefits to not procrastinating? Click/tap below to lrearn more.	
[TAB]		

Label	Content
Lower Stress and Anxiety	Research has shown that the longer we wait to get started on something, the more stress and anxiety we have. If instead you do something now, you remove the anxiety before it gets to you. [Design note: convey stress]
Higher Self-Discipline	Interestingly, research has shown that one of the biggest reasons people procrastinate is not only poor time management skills, but also because of poor self-discipline. Stopping the cycle automatically raises your self-discipline. [Design note: angst]
Better Work Outputs	Researchers also found that when students worked with less stress and anxiety and higher self-discipline, more feedback is sought, and work output is better. [Design note: happy young diverse person showing work output]

Figure 3.3 – Design document for the "Managing Yourself" course

We progressively get more detailed in addressing lower-order concerns in the *Tab* interaction, highlighting the benefits of *not procrastinating*. Additionally, we see that the types of interactions are called out in the left-hand column, while the design notes are called out in pink. The right-hand column is reserved for any additional explanations that the ID thinks they might need to add.

Depending on where you work, who's developing your course (you or another team), and/or the chosen software development tool, you might need to also provide a more detailed **storyboard** for your stakeholders before you go into development. We'll talk more about design documents and the storyboarding process in *Chapter 4, Creativity in Instructional Design.*

Glossary

A **storyboard** is like an even more detailed design document. It includes the text, visuals, and specific programming notes for an eLearning course. People choose to storyboard in different ways, some using Powerpoint, others using online tools like Miro or Mural.

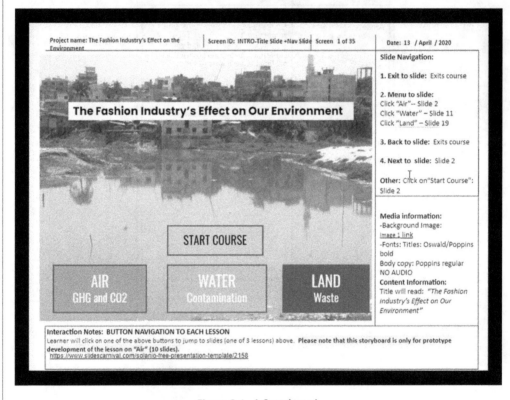

Figure 3.4 - A Storyboard

I never expected my first draft of a course outline or design document to translate well on screen or, for that matter, to be approved by my stakeholders. In fact, I absolutely expect not only to be making stakeholder revisions but a lot of my own revisions as well. There's a funny article that was written by the author Anne Lamott called *Sh!*#y First Drafts* that gave me great solace, I'll share it here (`https://bit.ly/3xpqfGc`).

Lamott's theory is that writers need to let go and know that their first draft will be somewhat like a *child's draft* – a bit disorganized and with a lot of romping around in your topic. The same concept can apply to writing for instructional design.

The idea is to just get started. Get all your crazy, disorganized ideas into somewhat of a semblance of a course structure via your content map and design document, and then revise, revise, and revise as you (and your stakeholders) see fit.

Pause and reflect

Being an instructional designer is not for the faint-hearted. Your work will be scrutinized, criticized, and revamped time and again by both you and your stakeholders. No matter how perfect you think your first design document is, rest assured, there *will* be changes!

Using concise wording and sentence structure

If you've come to instructional design from an academic background, your norm for *good* writing might be quite different from what's perceived to be acceptable writing for instructional design. While both academic writing and instructional design and writing are used to teach and inform, academic writing is used primarily in research-based scholarly journals, while instructional design writing is used to convey concepts in eLearning courses that will hopefully effect behavior change.

Usually, academic writing is written in the third person with a formal tone using complex sentence structure. instructional design projects are the opposite: they're most often written in a conversational tone, with excess words and phrases considered superfluous. In fact, the ability to simplify dense content down to about a 6th-grade reading comprehension level is a prized skill for any instructional designer.

Clarity and *conciseness* are the goals of instructional design writing. Often, the learner takes a course developed with interactions such as drag and drop, flashcards, accordions, tabs, and/or complex branch scenarios. As such, to avoid **cognitive overload** and keep the learner interested, it's important to keep the introductory text and instructions for these interactions clear and to the point (as seen in the preceding design document and storyboard examples).

Glossary

Cognitive overload happens when a learner has *too much information coming to them at once*. The term is derived from cognitive load theory, which builds on the premise that short-term (or working memory) has a limited capacity and that overloading reduces the ability of someone to learn.

Avoid filler phrases such as *As a matter of fact* or *In the event of*. This way, the learner will not only know exactly how to approach the interactivities you've designed into the course (for example, *select each card to learn more*), but they'll also be freed from extraneous information.

One way I check for clarity and conciseness in my writing is by reading out loud. This may or may not work for you, but this way, I find a lot of *too-big* words, redundancies, and awkward or wordy sentence construction issues.

> **Think about it**
>
> According to the seminal research done by Harvard and MIT psychology professor George Miller in the 1950s, a person's ability to hold different pieces of information in their short-term, or working, memory is limited to holding only seven plus or minus two bits of information.
>
> New research that considers today's device screen reading has reduced this number to just *four plus or minus two* pieces of information held in an average person's working memory.

The test

I've worked with a few global eLearning agencies, all of whom have giant, multinational corporations as their clients. Many of these larger agencies will ask a contract instructional designer to take an ID assessment before putting you on a contract. Nine out of ten times, that assessment will be partly, if not wholly, based on gauging your writing skills. Some of the concepts that will be tested include the following:

- Your ability to write in the active and passive voice

- How you're able to fix redundancies in writing

- Your knowledge of grammar and punctuation

Let's take a closer look at each of these concepts now.

Active versus passive voice

As we've just discussed, clear language is key when writing in instructional design. One way to improve your writing's effectiveness is to switch to writing in the *active voice* instead of the passive voice. Writing in the active voice is not only better writing, but also more action-oriented and engaging for your learner.

In active sentence construction, the subject of the sentence performs an action. In passive construction, the subject receives the action. In passive construction, the sentence is weakened by the subject not taking a direct action.

For example, consider the following:

- **Passive**: The book was written by Susan.

  Active: Susan wrote this book.

- **Passive**: A path of destruction was left by the hurricane.

  Active: The hurricane left a path of destruction.

- **Passive**: It was heard by me through the grapevine.

  Active: I heard it through the grapevine.

Simply put, the active voice just sounds better, especially when you want to speak to your audience with confidence and conviction and engage them to learn.

Writing without redundancies

Redundant writing happens when more words are included in a sentence than are needed to get your point across. Avoiding redundancy is important in ID writing, as online learners might read quickly or even skim the onscreen text. In ID writing, every word should have a purpose for being included in your sentence.

Let's look at some redundancy rewrites here:

- There is a possibility that the backup may not be successful.

  Rewrite: The backup may not be successful.

- Security must be increased to prevent violations.

  Rewrite: Increased security will prevent violations.

- The end result is exactly the same.

  Rewrite: The result is the same.

Another trap many people fall into is the use of unneeded words. The culprits that come to mind include words such as *very*, *really*, and *that*. Proofing your work to eliminate these redundant offenders will improve your writing's clarity.

Takeaway

Many eLearning agencies conduct word counts to gauge how long an online course will be based on average reading comprehension speeds and bill their clients accordingly. 180–200 **words per minute** or **WPM** are industry-standard onscreen reading speeds, while 130–150 WPM is a standard speed measure for voice-over/audio comprehension.

Restructuring sentences to avoid redundancies makes *less redundant writing* not only a clarity-of-writing conversation but a *money conversation* as well.

Grammar, punctuation, and typos

While this might seem like common sense, I often find common grammatical, punctuation, and spelling errors in finished, already-launched eLearning experiences (including my own). Yikes! There's nothing like a few typos and grammatical errors to immediately lose the learner's respect for a course that has been developed. When the learner's respect is lost, their engagement and motivation to complete the learning experience is lost, too.

While a comprehensive list of common typos and grammatical errors is impossible to include here, there are some common mistakes that I've found (and, frankly, periodically make myself) in online courses I've reviewed.

Here are the grammatical and punctuation errors I see most often in eLearning courses:

- **Over- or under-using commas**: Commas are meant for a few things, such as the following:

    - To separate two independent clauses (for example, parts of a sentence that can also stand alone)

    - After introductory phrases, words, and clauses such as *Moreover* or *Indeed*

    - After items in a list of three or more items, and in the case of using the Oxford comma, before the word *and* or *or* in such a list (for example, an Italian painter, sculptor, and architect)

> **Glossary**
> From the Oxford dictionary: *The Oxford comma is a comma used after the penultimate (last) item in a list of three or more items, before 'and' or 'or'.*

    Using commas outside the preceding uses is simply a superfluous use of the comma!

- **There versus Their versus They're**: *They're* is a contraction for *they are*, *their* refers to something owned by a group, and *there* refers to a place.

- **It's versus Its**: *Its* refers to the possessive form, while *it's* is the contraction for *it is*.

- **Your versus You're**: *Your* refers to ownership (for example, *Your car*), while *you're* is a contraction for *you are* (for example, *you're always on time!*).

- **Who versus Whom versus Whose versus Who's**: This is one of the trickier writing conventions in the English language. Let's break it down here:

    - *Who* identifies a living pronoun. For example, *who read the book?*

    - *Whom* describes someone who's receiving something, for example, *To whom do we send it?* Or it can be used to refer to someone on the receiving end of an action, for example, *Whom did we contract with to complete the project?*

    - *Whose* assigns ownership to someone. For example, *whose work shall we display?*

    - *Who's* is a contraction for *who is*. For example, *who's coming to the party?*

- **Affect versus Effect**: One is a verb that talks about change (*affect*), while the other is a noun about the result itself (*effect*). For example, *Ashley was affected by the hurricane* versus *The hurricane had devastating effects*.

- **Who versus That**: *Who* is used when you're describing a person. For example, *Kamlesh is someone who takes his work seriously*. *That* is used if you're describing an object; for example, *She picked up the phone that she found in the cinema*.

- **Capitalization errors in titles and headings**: These can differ based on a company's writing style guide. For example, some companies use all *sentence-case* words in their titles, except for the title's first word. However, in general, most title and heading *capitalization rules* are listed as follows:

  - The first word in the title/heading is capitalized.

  - Nouns, verbs (even *is*), adjectives, and proper nouns are also capitalized.

  - Articles, conjunctions, and prepositions are not capitalized.

- **Not correcting obvious typos and spelling errors**: No explanation is needed here – *check your work!*

Writing to motivate and engage

How to best engage a learner, especially in an independent, asynchronous eLearning environment, is an often discussed and investigated topic. In addition to self-reflective exercises, learner software interactions (drag and drop, flashcards, accordions, hotspots, and more), and knowledge checks, the way you write your course content plays a large role in how engaged your learners are with your course.

This section on motivating and engaging the learner wouldn't be complete without learning the basics of attention and retention in learning. According to neuroscience research (`https://bit.ly/3YzmgTp`), **a person's attention span only lasts for about 20 minutes** before needing some sort of change or refresher!

That said, the content in the courses we design needs to capture the learner's attention and hold it for at least 20 minutes.

Often, as IDs, we're charged with developing content for not-so-interesting topics to a target audience that we may or may not be entirely familiar with. Over time, I've found a few subtle writing hacks that help to hold a learner's attention longer (or at least that's what course survey results said!). These learner-engagement helpers include telling stories, inserting humor and the unexpected, and using copywriting techniques.

Tell stories

> *"Good stories do more than create a sense of connection. They build familiarity and trust and allow the listener to enter the story where they are, making them more open to learning."*
>
> *– Vanessa Boris, author, psychologist, professional storyteller, and executive coach*

People love a good story. One way to make dry, technical content more interesting is to turn it into a story. Research has shown that using stories in training courses allows us to better connect with and engage with the learner.

Research has also shown that storytelling makes learning *stickier* and enables the learner to both retain and retrieve information more easily. Some studies have found that *facts inserted into a story are 20 times more likely to be remembered than facts that are just stated* (`https://www.harvardbusiness.org/what-makes-storytelling-so-effective-for-learning/`). That's huge!

A common way to use storytelling in eLearning is by setting up a **short branch scenario** in which a character needs to solve a problem or issue in their workplace. These types of stories can be played out across various learner interactions, such as quiz/test questions, self-reflective discovery exercises, or software-driven branch scenario scenes.

Glossary

Developing **branching scenarios** is an interactive way to show content and test a learner's knowledge. According to Christy Tucker, a renowned branching scenario developer, in a branching scenario, learners make a series of decisions within a single situation. The learner can then observe whether they are comprehending the material based on the consequences of their choices.

So, how do we write these types of stories in learning experiences? Usually, stories encompass three components:

- A setup providing an environment where relatable-to-the-target-audience characters exist
- The problem that the main character or protagonist needs to solve (based on what you are trying to teach)
- The ability for the learner to help the main character to find the resolution – your teaching point

Depending on how long your scenario story is, there may even be plot twists or unforeseen consequences. Ideally, your learner can relate to the protagonist of your story on an emotional level; it's this emotional-level connection that makes the learning stickiest.

Inserting humor and the unexpected

Earlier in this chapter, we touched on the differences between academic and instructional design writing. One of these key differences is writing in an engaging, informal conversational tone in instructional design. But how do we do this?

There are a few simple methods you can use to make your writing more engaging. One of these is the use of **headlines**, not titles. Think about the titles of online articles you've read recently. How many times have you clicked on an article just because the headline was unexpected and maybe even sensational? Instead of coming up with routine course, lesson, and section headers, try incorporating these sorts of unexpected headlines instead.

One of my go-to clickbait websites is a blog called **Refinery 29**. Their editorial team does a great job of creating enticing headlines. I sometimes click on these headlines that are sent to me via email even though I have little to no interest in some of the topics.

For example, I would probably not have clicked on the articles *You Can Get These Disney Gifts (For Adults) Without Wishing Upon A Star* or *Influencing Is The Dream Job—But Is It Really Worth It?* if they had been called *Disney Gifts for Adults* or *The Downsides of Being an Influencer*. I'm not suggesting using all sensational titles in the next course you design, but certainly, adding some interest to your titles motivates the learner to press on!

Another way to get a learner's attention is to incorporate humorous blurbs, quotes, call-out statements, or questions in your courses. These might be similar to the conversational tone Google uses to tell users we no longer have access to a file (*Aw snap. Something went wrong with your access*), or what might be used in the copy of an e-commerce site.

You can intersperse these call-out blurbs, quotes, and questions throughout your course to garner more curiosity from your learners. Here's an example question from a management course I created that was designed to pique the learner's interest:

How could your life improve if you could manage these people better?

By inserting a *What's in it for me?* question, we're able to lure the learner back into the content – especially if they're veering toward that 20-minute attention span zone-out.

Here's another blurb example that I placed before a branch scenario interaction:

Monica doesn't like giving feedback to the team. Learn what the team thinks of her management style.

Simply using humor can also effectively reel the learner's attention back in. For example, in Articulate Rise™ software, you can *gate* your lessons by not allowing the learner to move on to the next lesson if they haven't finished the content. Instead of using the default software message, which reads something like *Please complete all content above before moving on*, try something like the following:

Why so fast? Finish all of the content above (we promise it won't be boring).

Not only will your learners smile, but they'll also know a human created their course, which might make them feel more connected.

Borrowing from copywriters

Friends of mine in the marketing world have told me there's a method called **AIDA**, which is used for writing website and advertising copy. I think there is a lot that instructional designers can take from this technique. If you think about it, our goal as instructional designers is not only to engage via our writing, but also to make sure that the people who take our course change their behavior and learn new concepts. In this regard, persuasive writing in instructional design is helpful.

AIDA stands for the following:

- **Attention**: Grabbing your target learner audience's attention by calling out something relevant to them.
- **Interest**: Holding their interest through interesting facts, statistics, or even use cases.
- **Desire**: Emphasizing the benefits of what you're teaching. Show them how their life (or a task) will be better if they change their behavior.
- **Action**: Providing a call to action or some sort of proposal. This can be encouraging someone to try out a new method of doing something, signing up for another course, reading an article, or watching a video to learn more.

> Takeaway
>
> Write for learner engagement by thinking of ways to write *differently*. Incorporate relevant-to-the-topic stories, humor, the unexpected, and the AIDA model for persuasive writing.

Help! I've been asked to write a video script

As an instructional designer, there's a very good chance you'll be asked to write video scripts, as videos are almost always part of a learning experience. The thought of scripting someone, or, worse, scripting for animation may indeed freak you out a bit if you don't consider yourself a creative writer. Read on to learn some tips.

What is scriptwriting in instructional design?

Your job in scriptwriting for ID is just like any other scriptwriter: you need to entertain. In writing that's "heard" and "watched" versus writing that's "read", there are some key differences:

- Audio scripts really need to spark the learner's imagination and draw them into your content. Here's where reading your content out loud comes in handy: you need to pay attention to the sounds and cadence of the words you choose and the phrases you write.
- Less is more! Professional voiceover artists are expensive and often charge by the word, so the adage **Keep It Simple Stupid** (**KISS**) applies here. Only use the words you need to convey your message. Take breaks from your scriptwriting for a few hours, come back, and re-read it aloud. This will allow you to continue pruning extraneous content and/or difficult-to-read words or phrases.

Remember,writing for video storyboards should go hand-in-hand with choosing video reference images. It's easier to be explicit and literal when you're working off a reference image or a relevant statistical slide.

Use case – the writing (in)competency

In this section, I'm including a real-world use case that highlights the importance of writing in ID by looking at the many edits needed for one of my client's eLearning courses. You'll be able to see where *the writing competency* comes into play in the development of an Articulate Storyline e-learning course.

As the owner of a small eLearning agency, I sometimes need to hire contract instructional designers. I like to offer recent graduates or those who are trying to pivot into instructional design these opportunities to help them secure their first projects for their portfolios, just as others helped me at the beginning of my ID career.

As a former instructor, I tend to give my contractors a lot of direction on these projects, specifically, nuances about the client's voice and tone preferences.

When I first started hiring contractors, I didn't assess potential hires' writing skills. Like many IDs, I was wowed by portfolios and course demos of highly technical Articulate software interactions or cool video development.

However, I quickly learned that even though an ID might have superb software authoring development skills, their writing skills could be severely lacking. In fact, I now give every ID I speak to a short writing assessment, which you'll find at the end of this chapter.

So, onto the case story at hand. Remember the grammar, punctuation, and sentence construction points that I mentioned in the first section of this chapter? On one learning project, a recent grad ID I hired needed help in **all** of these areas. That's correct – all of their writing had concerns, specifically the following:

- The course outline provided did not follow a logical sequence or flow of higher-order to lower-order information. A learner would get lost.

- After sorting through the course structure issues, I found that most sentences were redundant with words such as *very*, *really*, and *that* overly used. In fact, the overall sentence construction was awkward and redundant and included lots of phrases such as *small in size* and *basic fundamentals*.

- Pretty much all the common grammatical and punctuation error rules cited in this chapter were broken from *their/they're* to *its/it's*, and more.

- The mandatory client writing voice was largely ignored. This was a project for a large corporation that dictated all their learning be written in this very specific style. For example, this client preferred contractions, sentence-case titles and headings, and a young yet intelligent voice. Instead, the written course content contained no contractions, capitalized titles and headings, and used a formal, third-person voice!

While the ID did a nice job selecting and developing the learning interactions in Articulate Storyline, the course was essentially unnavigable due to its writing errors. Moreover, it would have been promptly rejected by the client due to not being written in their corporate voice. After recommending several edits that were only somewhat completed, I ended up paying the contractor what was owed and revising the whole course myself.

In thinking about this project, it would have been a lot more costly and time efficient for me to write and design a detailed storyboard on my own and then send it to an Articulate developer, rather than to rely on an ID with poor writing skills to write, design, and develop the course.

Needless to say, this project stayed in beginning the alpha phase of development longer than anticipated and was delivered late due to the many unforeseen basic writing revisions that were needed. If you think writing is not your thing, consider hiring a copywriter for your next writing-intensive project or video scripts and tackling the course development yourself.

> **Glossary**
>
> The **alpha** phase/prototype in eLearning represents the first stab at developing a course in whichever software authoring tool is chosen.
>
> Usually, most or all multimedia resources, graphics, interactions, and written content are inserted in the alpha prototype. The alpha version is then reviewed by stakeholders (internal, external, and SMEs) to get their feedback and revised into the next iteration, which is called the **beta**.
>
> The final product, which is either launched directly or sent for user testing, is typically called the **gold** product.

Building your writing competency

Congratulations! You've completed an important chapter in this book and now understand the importance of being a capable writer in the field of instructional design.

Once again, this final section of your chapter is designed to offer you some additional thoughts and resources surrounding building your writing competency. Whether you love or are indifferent to writing, you should be able to find something here that will help you to hone your craft.

Building your skills toward writing more concisely

Writing concisely in instructional design saves you and your stakeholders time and money. One great source that will help you with clarity and conciseness in your writing is the app **Grammarly**™ (https://www.grammarly.com/). The basic account level is free and is definitely worth the three minutes it will take you to sign up – especially if you're an instructional designer.

Moreover, if you work for an organization without a style guide, Grammarly has just introduced the ability to create a company style guide like many large corporations already have. This is a great way to help your organization improve the consistency of its voice and style, as well as set grammar and punctuation rules that everyone on the team will know to follow.

Another great resource for checking for English language redundancy conventions (and writing in general) is Writing Commons (`https://writingcommons.org/article/writing-concisely-and-avoiding-redundancy/`). The linked article takes a deeper dive into the common redundancy traps and is a great one to bookmark for future reference.

Fellow instructional designer Devlin Peck has a great video on writing in ID entitled *Top 5 Writing Tips for Instructional Designers* (`https://www.youtube.com/watch?v=0zUVEmGA-OM`). In it, he takes a closer look at the use of conversational tone, using the active voice, showing not telling, using commas correctly, and using simple language. If there's one of these areas you feel like you still need a bit more context and how-to, check out this short video.

Lastly, if you need more tips and tricks to help you learn how to remove redundant content from your writing, check out this article from Articulate's E-Learning Heroes blog (`https://community.articulate.com/articles/how-to-remove-redundant-e-learning-course-text`).

In it, the author highlights easy ways to remove redundancies with examples for not repeating yourself, reconstructing sentences, shortening phrases into words, getting rid of filler phrases, and removing unnecessary words.

Building your storytelling skills

We've covered several ways you can increase learner engagement in your eLearning writing earlier in the chapter, such as incorporating relevant stories and incorporating humor and the unexpected. Instructional designer Connie Malamed takes a deeper dive into engaging the learner through writing in the article named *Supercharge Your Writing for Instructional Design* (`https://theelearningcoach.com/elearning_design/supercharge-your-writing-for-instructional-design/`).

In this article, she discusses finding the right voice, how to write a headline, writing teasers, developing your story's protagonist, writing microcopy, and in general, adding personality to your eLearning courses.

As we discussed previously, perhaps the best way to both engage your audience and ensure that your learning sticks is to create a story. Stories help learners to remember, inspire action, and shift beliefs and behavior patterns.

In the TED video *Business Storytelling Made Easy* (`https://www.youtube.com/watch?v=WKIZ0bicfFw&t=2s`), master storyteller Kelly Parker discusses the basics of storytelling to a business audience. She dissects the importance of knowing your target learner audience's problem before you set up your story.

She then examines the importance of painting a picture with distinguishable things your audience can relate to. Lastly, she emphasizes the importance of *the proposal* and *giving before you ask*. Although Ms. Parker is not an instructional designer, it's a great video that teaches you a step-by-step technique for creating a story, so please check it out!

There's also a great book written by Hadiya Nuriddin called *Storytraining*, which outlines various ways to incorporate storytelling into your training courses. While it's primarily oriented toward storytelling at in-person training events, many of the concepts can be easily translated into live online training events and even asynchronous eLearning courses.

Building your persuasive writing style with AIDA

As we discussed in the *Borrow from copywriters* section of this chapter, our job as IDs is to effect behavior change toward the ultimate organizational goal of improving performance. This involves writing persuasively and, essentially, convincing the learner to change their beliefs and behaviors, making marketing's AIDA model (attention, interest, desire, and action) uniquely applicable.

This video (`https://www.youtube.com/watch?v=flgSOV9bW4k`) from Neville Medhora, creator of *The Copywriting Course*, outlines a simple method to help you learn to use this model in your writing. He gives many examples of persuasive pitches that, while oriented toward selling a service or product, with a little creativity, you could use toward presenting new course concepts.

Building your overall writing skills

As promised, I'm including an ID writing assessment for you to take to gauge your own grammar and punctuation skills (hopefully, you'll ace it after reading this chapter!). To tie back to some of your previous learning from *Chapter 1, Welcome to Your New Career*, I've also included a section on writing actionable LOs. Suggested answers are available in the *Appendices* section at the end of the book. Good luck!

The ID writing assessment

I hope this ID writing assessment not only helps you to gauge your writing skills but also to land your next ID role. If you're someone who is an independent ID like me, feel free to reproduce these questions in any way, shape, or form to suit your business needs.

Activity 1 | Measurable LOs

Which of the following instructional goals/LOs is measurable? Answer *yes* if you think it is, or *no* if you don't. Then, rewrite the learning goals you don't think are measurable into something that is meaningful and measurable for the learner:

- Learners will review videos and attend lectures on future trends in medicine. (Yes/No)

- Learners will select examples of the concept of a growth mindset from a list of examples and non-examples. (Yes/No)
- Learners will understand the procedure for applying for a job. (Yes/No)
- Learners will administer an allergy injection. (Yes/No)
- Learners will compute the mean, range, and standard deviation of a series of ten numbers. (Yes/No)
- Learners will have acquired the ability to deal with conflict. (Yes/No)

Activity 2 | Passive versus Active voice

Try your hand at rewriting the following sentences from *passive* to *active* voice:

- **Passive**: The book is being read by most of the class.

  Active: _____.
- **Passive**: By then, the soundtrack will have been completely remixed by the sound engineers.

  Active: _____.
- **Passive**: The user interface can be accessed from the desktop.

  Active: _____.
- **Passive**: If you have questions, I can be reached at 555 555-5555.

  Active: _____.
- **Passive**: A path of destruction was left by the twister.

  Active: _____.
- **Passive**: Menu items can be added to existing OneClick menus.

  Active: _____.
- **Passive**: The entrance exam was failed by one-third of the applicants.

  Active: _____.

Activity 3 | Redundancies

Rewrite each sentence to avoid redundancy without changing its meaning:

- There is a possibility that the backup may not be successful.

  Rewrite: _____.
- Security must be increased in order to prevent violations.

  Rewrite: _____.

- The end result is exactly the same.

  Rewrite: _____.

- The majority of applications ran smoothly, taking into consideration the high risk.

  Rewrite: _____.

- With better advance planning, we can improve our current status.

  Rewrite: _____.

- Results recorded over a period of time showed that CD-ROM discs were not suitable for this purpose.

  Rewrite: _____.

Activity 4 | Typos and spelling

Rewrite the following sentences without any typos. If you've already downloaded Grammarly or another similar tool, try not to use it!

If you think about it, their is alot of data transferring on the sever. Because we do not have enough hard disc space, the only solution is to simply the amount of data that users need to excess. We will provides the documentation for this training, rather then having it done internally. There for, we must setup some log ins for our employees. We will need to altar some of the privileges so that vitally information does not leek.

Summary

I hope this chapter has brought to light the importance of *writing in instructional design*. If after reading this chapter, you've self-assessed that you're already a great writer, congratulations! You need now only continue the good work.

For many people, at least *some* of the writing for instructional design concepts we've covered in this chapter will be new. The great news is that you now have the knowledge and resources to build your ID writing competency **before** continuing in your career and making these common mistakes (like most of us do!). Remember, writing can comprise up to 80% of a given ID project, so bravo to you for proactively honing your skills.

You've now discovered the first two ID competencies and are already halfway through this short book! In the next chapter, we'll discuss the third ID capability: **The Creativity Competency**.

4

Creativity in Instructional Design

"You can't use up creativity. The more you use, the more you have."

– Maya Angelou

Creativity means different things to a lot of people. In this chapter, we'll whittle creativity down from an ethereal (and sometimes daunting) concept to a within-grasp, daily practice.

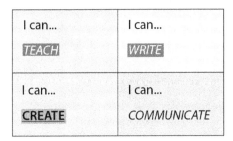

Figure 4.1 – The Four Competencies Model

In this chapter, we'll review:

- The meaning of creativity
- Ways to develop your creativity – and why it's important in instructional design
- Creativity as applied to instructional design and creative problem solving
- A real-world design thinking use case
- Resources to help you to continue to build your creativity

What does being 'creative' mean

When we think of creativity, often, we think of someone good with color, who can paint or draw, has lots of ideas, or, in some way, shape, or form, has a unique approach to things. While it's true these are all aspects of creativity, they can also mean something different in the context of instructional design.

Like many other creative fields, instructional design is surprisingly analytical and creative at once. While you, as an ID, might have many original and interesting ideas surrounding how to approach a given learning experience, there will most likely be some organizational constraints surrounding what you can and cannot do. For example, you'll need to ensure your content and interaction design supports all the course learning objectives, even if you did not write them.

Additionally, you'll be constrained by the learning experience's requested length, its preferred delivery modality, and possibly, an organization's mandated look and feel or voice. Meeting all these requirements while still delivering an innovative learning experience puts an ID into both the creative and analytical camps at once.

In instructional design, creativity is largely centered around the ability to develop innovative ideas and perspectives and problem-solve. Although visual graphics and well-designed learner interactions are important – and we will discuss them in this chapter – creativity in instructional design is less about artistic expression and more about *innovation and creative problem-solving in instructional design*. Your job is to sell your content to your learner – and get them to adapt and change their behavior. This takes creativity!

> *"Creativity is defined as the tendency to generate or recognize ideas, alternatives, or possibilities that may be useful in solving problems, communicating with others, and entertaining ourselves and others."*
>
> *– Robert E. Franken, Professor Emeritus at the University of Calgary and author of Human Motivation*

Can creativity be developed?

First, let's start with *why* someone should try to improve their creativity. According to Brad Hokanson, a professor of graphic design and creative problem-solving at the University of Minnesota, *Creativity is three times stronger than intelligence* in terms of recognizing career and personal achievement throughout one's lifetime, (`https://bit.ly/3ItXGOs`). This is an impetus to work on your creativity!

People assume they're not creative because they weren't "born that way." Society, our educational system, and even our families tend to pigeonhole us as we're growing up; sadly, sometimes along gender lines ("She's so creative!" or "He's so good at math!"). Not only is this unfortunate, but it's also incorrect.

Much research shows that an individual can learn to be more creative – especially in the areas of innovation and creative problem-solving. While certainly, some people have more propensity toward creative skills in, say, fine arts or music than others, experts argue that **building creativity is like building a muscle**: *one must learn to use their creativity to make it strong* (`https://knowledge.wharton.upenn.edu/article/can-creativity-be-taught/`).

Even for naturally creatively gifted people, a considerable time investment must be made to become great at something. This research shows us that *creativity can be nurtured through learning, experiences, and most importantly, practice*:

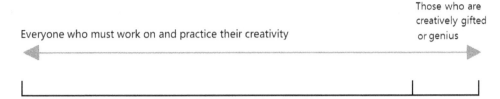

Those who are
creatively gifted
or genius

Everyone who must work on and practice their creativity

Figure 4.2 – The creativity continuum

"In any population, basically the distribution of creativity follows the normal curve. At the absolute extreme, you have Einstein and Picasso, and you don't have to teach them – they are the geniuses. Nearly everyone else in the distribution, and the type of people you would deal with at leading universities and companies, can learn creativity."

– Jerry (Yoram) Wind, Professor of Marketing, The Wharton School of the University of Pennsylvania

Pause and reflect
Where do you think **you** fall on the creativity continuum? Why?

Five science-backed ways to develop your general creativity

We've established that to some degree, creativity may be innate. However, we've also learned research shows that creativity can be nurtured and developed. Here are some ways research has shown to develop and maintain your *creative muscle*.

1. Being open to experience

Science tells us that the most prevalent trait of people who score highly on creative personality assessments was the ability to be *open to experience* (http://bit.ly/3RZiosw). According to researchers, "open to experience" means being open to variety, being intellectually curious, having an active imagination, being in touch with your emotions, and having an appreciation for aesthetics.

The good news here is that with intention and practice, we can all become more open to experience, thus more innovation-minded and creative. This practice could include traveling to unfamiliar places, learning a new language, trying a crossword puzzle, or simply meeting new people. Varying your life experiences and increasing your tolerance for different people, places, and things will help you to develop more ideas, be more intellectually curious, and in turn, become more creative.

2. Using your emotions to spark innovation

Researchers have found that being attuned to *your feelings and emotions is* another personality trait found in people who tested at a high level on creativity scales. Many of the world's most creative innovations have come from an *emotional* place; for example, an inventor who's bothered or frustrated by something, or another who loves or enjoys something so much that they feel compelled to bring it to others.

Consider the following:

- Jaap Haartsen created Bluetooth technology because he was *frustrated* by being wired while running.
- Kristina Johnson and Gary Sharp *loved* creating holograms as students; together, they invented the technology that ultimately created digital 3D movies.
- Aproova Mehta *hated* grocery shopping. He created Instacart, one of the first online grocery shopping platforms, to combat this.

The global design and innovation firm IDEO (`https://www.ideo.com/about`) incorporates emotions into its problem-solving sessions by using something it calls the *I like but I wish* exercise. In this emotionally charged technique, brainstorming participants develop lists of *I like but I wish* statements for a specific problem to drive change and foster innovation. For example, circling back to grocery shopping, *I like but I wish* statements might sound something like this:

- **I like** *grocery shopping,* **but I wish** *I didn't have to wait in long checkout lines.*
- **I like** *grocery shopping,* **but I wish** *I didn't have to run errands in addition to shopping (that is, to the bank, dry cleaners, or drug store).*
- **I like** *grocery shopping,* **but I wish** *the self-checkout machines would work for all types of merchandise – and not stop working.*

From these emotional *I like but I wish* statements, we can see where many innovations have sprung up: automated self-checkout, the inclusion of more services in supermarkets, and improved self-checkout such as that of Amazon's Go stores.

3. Developing an appreciation for aesthetics

According to the American Society for Aesthetics (`https://aesthetics-online.org/`), the term *aesthetics* is understood to include all studies of the arts and related types of experience from a philosophic, scientific, or another theoretical standpoint, including those of psychology, sociology, anthropology, cultural history, art criticism, and education.

The arts include visual arts, literature, music, and theater arts. *Related types of experience* include alternative design forms, such as graphic, fashion, or even interior design.

> **Think about it**
> Would you rather look at a pile of haphazardly thrown books on the floor, or neatly color-coded
> books on a shelf? Aesthetics are more important than we realize!

Do you need to become a card-carrying member of the aesthetics society to build your creativity?
Absolutely not. But by developing an appreciation for all art and design forms, you're developing
your creativity by learning to examine and think about art and design from different perspectives.

4. Being comfortable with ambiguity

According to Hokanson, people with higher levels of creativity are also **comfortable with ambiguity**.
They're able to keep multiple foci – meaning that they are comfortable with having not just one, but
maybe two or three ideas at the same time toward solving a given problem. They're not *single-track*
thinkers. Creative thinkers enjoy taking risks to move an idea forward and are comfortable doing so.

Being comfortable with ambiguity helps the creative problem-solving process. You learn to become
more flexible in your decision-making processes (for example, we could try *this*, or we could try *that*).

At IDEO, a culture of ambiguity is embraced. Some of the ways the IDEO design team navigates
ambiguity are listed as follows:

- **Plan NOT to know**: The next time you're faced with a question you don't really know the answer
  to say, "I don't know - yet". While this might be difficult at first, vulnerability builds trust – and
  you'll appear calm in the face of uncertainty.

- **Shift "should" to "could"**: Remember that the word *should* suggests only *one* way forward – a
  creativity killer. *Could*, on the other hand, is a platform for generating new ideas.

- **Change the context**: If you find you're stuck, simply move away from your screen and do
  something else for a while. This will lower your anxiety and force you to physically, mentally,
  and emotionally change the context of what you're working on. By focusing on something else,
  you'll bring a fresh perspective to the problem.

5. Continuing to creatively learn and grow

Adopting a **growth mindset** is the key to maintaining and building curiosity. The concept of a growth
mindset is the result of decades of research conducted by psychologist Carol Dweck (`https://
fs.blog/carol-dweck-mindset/`) and her colleagues at Stanford University. People who
believe their talents can be developed through hard work, ongoing learning, good strategies, and input
from others have a growth mindset. Those who adopt a growth mindset continue to seek opportunities
to learn and improve throughout their lives.

Ongoing, lifetime learning sparks creativity. Learning new things builds upon your existing experiences and curiosity and can stimulate your imagination. However, we're not talking about memorizing facts but more about creative learning. *Learning in a creative way is about developing skills and knowledge that you can apply to your work as a designer.*

For example, I took a series of IDEO design thinking courses to learn how to improve my creative problem-solving ability. I not only learned a new method of brainstorming but have been able to apply design thinking techniques to specific ID projects. By using the design thinking method, I've been able to better address my client's needs by developing more innovative learning solutions to solve their specific problems. Add last sentence: More about design thinking in instructional design in a few!

As IDs, it's also important to keep learning not only about instructional design but also about related design areas.

Some other related areas to continue your learning might include the following:

Growing your visual design skills

So much of what we accomplish as learning designers is through visual representation. If you don't have a visual arts or design background, one area for creative learning and growth might be visual design. Visual design includes relevant images, videos, and graphics such as flowcharts, diagrams, graphs, and illustrations.

Interactivities that can be developed in eLearning authoring software, such as simulations, flashcards, hot spots, or drag and drop interactions, may also be considered a form of visual information and design.

The visual elements that we create or choose for our courses, such as downloadable job aids, videos, and presentations improve learner engagement and comprehension. Not only do visuals add aesthetic interest to a learning experience, but research shows that *75% of information processed by the brain is from some sort of visual format*. Visuals are also better mapped in learners' minds than only text (`https://bit.ly/3lxtRmN`).

There are some easy ways to improve your visual design skills. For starters, you can learn about the **basic principles of design**, such as balance, rhythm, line, emphasis, contrast, unity, and (visual) texture. It's also important to learn a bit about **basic color theory** (hue versus saturation versus tint), the differences between Pantone, Hex, and RGB color codes, and how they're used.

Lastly, take it upon yourself to learn a bit about different font families and **typography**. The fonts you choose for your learning experiences will also play a significant role in how your visual design represents the look and feel of the organization you're designing for.

Stretching your knowledge of UX/UI design

Instructional designers are, by and large, designing in the digital space, so it's important to learn a bit about related fields, such as **Human-Computer Interaction** (**HCI**) and **User Experience/Interface Design** (**UX/UI**). Knowing basic UX/UI principles will help you understand how your learners process digital visual information.

Becoming familiar with the basic tenets of UX and UI design, such as *Miller's, Fitt's, and Hick's Laws* (`https://lawsofux.com/`) will improve the way you design your courses by understanding how people approach and mentally process digital experiences.

Growing your knowledge of inclusive and universal design

As designers, we need to ensure that any type of learner can access, navigate, and learn from the experiences we design. **Universal Design for Learning (UDL)** (`https://udlguidelines.cast.org/`), is the idea that learning should be inclusive and available to *all* learners regardless of how they learn. This means designing your courses both in terms of accessibility and learning styles, with the goal of providing flexible options for learners of all types. Originally created to help teach students with disabilities, such as attention deficit disorder, or other neuro-diversities, UDL is now used in general population curricula and learning experiences.

Closely related to UDL is the concept of **course accessibility**. This includes designing your courses to address common physical disabilities, such as low vision or hearing loss. Concepts include the use of high color contrast, image alt tags, video closed captioning to address hearing loss, or font that is readable for low vision.

Accessibility and UDL alike also include softer inclusive design concepts such as ensuring consistent navigation, offering content in multiple modalities and expressions, and designing course interactions with accessibility in mind.

To recap...

Hopefully, this section has given you some inspiration for developing and building your general creative muscle by being more open to experience, using emotions to spark innovation, developing an appreciation for the aesthetic, and becoming more comfortable with ambiguity. Now let's pivot to building the creativity type that will most help you in your instructional design practice: *creative problem-solving*.

Creative problem-solving in instructional design

This section will help you to learn how to apply your creativity to problem-solving in instructional design. Remember, creativity in ID often means thinking out of the box and helping your organization or client innovate and problem-solve. **Your job as a learning designer is to find novel and applicable learning solutions**. Often, this means that you will be going through an iterative, always-improving process in your work. This is creative problem-solving!

If you and your stakeholders have a new problem, you'll obviously need to find new and different solutions. You can't keep doing the same thing if there's an entirely new problem. You'll need to brainstorm ideas that are *creative solutions* – otherwise, all you'll get is incremental (or mediocre) change.

Ask yourself the following questions when tasked with a new problem:

- How might the problem be addressed differently?
- How many innovative ideas can I come up with? *Aim for at least 10.*
- How might a better solution be applied, based on these ideas?
- How might I try out different alternatives in terms of what's possible and what everybody else already knows?

> *"It's a three-step process. If it's something that you've done all the time, it's probably not creative in terms of the challenges we're given. If it's something that looks a little bit unusual to you and it's rare or unique, that's sort of in the middle range, and if it's something that you've never seen before and it solves the problem, that's really something that's much more creative."*
>
> *– Brad Hokanson, professor of graphic design and creative problem-solving*

In an article called *Creativity in the training and practice of instructional designers: the Design/Creativity Loop model*, authors and researchers Gregory Clinton and Brad Hokanson cite the creative problem-solving process as an *iterative loop* that includes the following:

- Learning problem identification
- Brainstorming preparation
- Idea generation, or incubation
- Identifying the most valuable ideas, or illumination
- Development and testing, or elaboration and verification

The iterative aspect comes when the idea does not work as well as perceived, and adjustments are made. This is why creative problem-solving is visualized as a loop, not a straight line. You might end up making small adjustments or even starting all over. Clinton and Hokanson call this process the **Design/Creativity Loops** model (the **DCL** model):

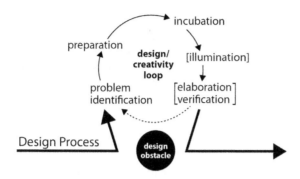

Figure 4.3 – The DCL model (Clinton and Hokanson, 2011)

In their research, Clinton and Hokanson cleverly layer their DCL model of creative problem-solving onto the **ADDIE model** – the **Analysis, Design, Development, Implementation, and Evaluation** phases of instructional design.

- **A (Analysis)**: This is the phase in which the *identification of the design problem/project* is made. Target learners are identified, and the objectives and goals for behavior change are established. During these initial information-gathering phases, project constraints are identified and the design problem is further defined.

- **D (Design)**: This is the brainstorming, incubation, and *diverging of ideas* for the learning experience. In this phase, as many ideas as contextually possible are presented. Design decisions are made about media and modality, specific instructional strategies, and the aesthetic look and feel of the course.

- **D (Development)**: This is elaborating on the many ideas presented during the design phase, then *converging ideas toward the illumination of the ideas that hold the highest value* for the learning experience. These ideas are then developed into the project's initial *alpha* prototype.

- **I (Implementation)**: Here, the alpha prototype is reviewed by **subject matter experts (SMEs)** and stakeholders. At this point, the SME and stakeholder review should include reviewing software functionality, content, visual aesthetics, and branding. Feedback on necessary changes is made, and the alpha prototype is iterated upon to the *beta* stage. A similar review process continues until the desired learning experience is achieved and the *gold*, or final product, is delivered. *The learning experience is then launched.*

- **E (Evaluation)**: In this final phase, the overall effectiveness of instruction is *evaluated and verified*. This may include formative (during the learning experience) or summative (after the experience) assessments. Additionally, organizations may want to track learner performance over time to assess for true behavior change. If the evaluation/assessment finds that the original problem is not well-solved, then the *iterative creative problem-solving loop starts again.*

> **Glossary**
>
> Creative problem-solving includes two types of thinking: **divergent** and **convergent**. Divergent thinking is finding original and novel answers, while convergent thinking is finding a solution that's contextually valuable. Convergent thinking is the evaluation and verification of ideas – for example, *Will this work?*

Hopefully, aligning Clinton and Hokanson's DCL model with the popular ADDIE instructional design model helps you to conceptualize how creative problem-solving applies to instructional design – not just in ADDIE's *design* phase but throughout the entire ADDIE process.

Design thinking for creative problem solving

Design thinking is gaining popularity as a framework for problem-solving in instructional design. Design thinking is a human-centered approach to creative problem-solving that was developed by IDEO in conjunction with Stanford University's Hasso Platner Institute of Design, or **d.school**.

This highly structured form of brainstorming plays on the use of *human emotion* in the design process – specifically, *empathy*. Like Clinton and Hokanson's creative DCL model for creative problem-solving, design thinking is an *iterative process* that looks to find creative solutions through fully understanding and empathizing with the end user or learner. In design thinking, you are literally putting yourself in your learner's shoes.

There are five stages of the design thinking process after a problem has been identified: 1) empathize, 2) define, 3) ideate, 4) prototype, and 5) test:

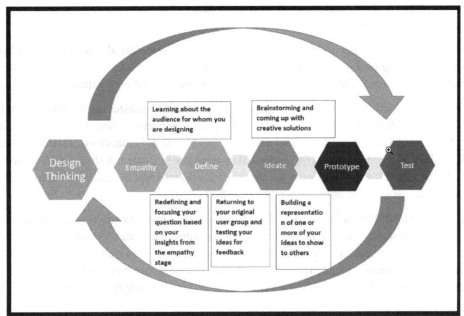

Figure 4.4 – The design thinking process (https://creativecommons.org/licenses/by-sa/4.0/)

- **Phase I: Empathize**: Empathy is central to the human-centered design process. This is where you will strive to better understand your learners' and stakeholders' thoughts and motivations about the problem at hand and within the context of your design challenge. The empathy stage involves you conducting primary research by *observing* your target learning audience (users), *engaging and asking them questions*, and *watching and listening* while they walk and talk you through the tasks that are relevant to your problem. Through this first-hand research, you become better equipped to understand how the problem is currently being handled and what's important to them.

  The empathy phase in the design thinking process is so important that designers using this method even create separate **empathy maps**. Empathy mapping helps you to get your findings out of your head and onto a wall or into a digital brainstorming tool, such as Google Jamboard, Miro, or Jira. You can start to make connections by posting interview quotes, diagrams of the users' journeys, or even images. You'll then divide them into four quadrants by what your end users (learners/stakeholders) *say, do, think, and feel*: (please see the example of a completed empathy map in this chapter's Use Case). Organizing what you've learned in your empathetic interviews will help you to process and synthesize the information you've just gleaned from your end users.

- **Phase II: Define**: Here, you will frame the problem based on what you've learned about your learners and stakeholders and the context. The end goal at this stage is to *develop a meaningful and actionable* **problem statement** that focuses on the needs and insights of a particular user (or a combination of the users' needs and insights). Create your problem statement by combining the user, need, and insight to effectively work through the rest of your design work. According to the Stanford d.school, an effective problem statement should do the following:

  - Focus on and frame the problem

  - Inspire your team/stakeholders

  - Inform criteria for evaluating competing ideas

  - Empower your team to make decisions independently in parallel

  - Capture the hearts and minds of people you meet

  - Be well-scoped and specific, not broad

  After you define your problem statement, a great way to move forward to the ideate phase is to develop a list of *How-Might-We . . .?* brainstorming questions derived from your problem statement.

- **Phase III: Ideate**: Ideation is the idea-generation phase of the design thinking process. Here, you are *generating/brainstorming as many relevant concepts as possible*, **diverging** in your creative thinking. The ideas generated at this stage will supply the source material for building prototype(s) and getting your alpha solution(s) into the hands of your stakeholders.

  There are many ideation techniques such as body storming (putting yourself in the user's shoes through role-play), mind mapping, and even sketching your ideas. It's important to note that judgment needs to be deferred at this stage of the process; you are not yet evaluating ideas. Encourage brainstorming participants to be as imaginative (not rational) as possible during the ideation phase!

At the conclusion of your ideation session, choose three voting criteria (IDEO suggests *the most likely to delight, the rational choice, and the most unexpected*) to **converge** down to three different ideas generated during brainstorming.

Carry the three ideas that receive the most votes forward into rough prototyping. This is a different approach from carrying just one idea forward and is not only diplomatic, but it will help with options and innovation in the next phase of the process.

- **Phase IV: Prototype**: Prototyping involves building lo-fi/rough prototypes that can be made in minutes for evaluation, then iterating toward a more polished, hi-fi prototype. As instructional designers, we can think of this as the pre-alpha (storyboarding) and alpha phases of ID development.

  Prototyping is important as it allows us to *effectively communicate our ideas to stakeholders* and start a directed conversation with stakeholders and possibly end users (learners). The lower-fi your initial prototypes are, the less time you spend iterating based on feedback (and committing to a specific direction early on).

  Early and simple prototypes also allow the ID to break down a large problem into testable, smaller chunks. Additionally, prototyping allows you to enter the *test* phase earlier. This is especially relevant in terms of testing the functionality of customized ID course prototypes developed in web-authoring software programs such as Articulate Storyline.

  "If a picture is worth a thousand words, a prototype is worth a thousand pictures."

  – Stanford d.school

- **Phase V: Test**: From an ID lens, this is where we've moved into the beta development phase and are ready to test our product. To continue the human-centric/empathetic design model, you might want to consider a test run with a small group of learners to see what their experience is like with your instructional product. It's key to *put your polished, "beta" prototype in front of end users* (your target learner audience), not just your stakeholders.

  We test to refine prototypes and solutions, learn more about our target audience, and refine our point of view. After learner testing, you might find that your solution is not right, and maybe even that you didn't frame your problem correctly to start with.

  A hallmark of design thinking is **iteration**. As an aspiring instructional designer, you're probably well-familiar with iteration. Here, the difference is that iteration is baked into the design thinking process: it's expected that for each problem you're solving, you will cycle through the preceding process multiple times or perhaps within a specific step – such as creating multiple prototypes. When I use the design thinking process, I think of iteration almost as its own step. I assume iteration will happen – even after the gold course product is launched.

"A rule of thumb: always prototype as if you know you're right, but test as if you know you're wrong. Testing is the chance to refine your solutions and make them better."

– Stanford d.school

The more you practice the design thinking process in your ID practice, the easier and more useful it will become. After a few cycles, you'll learn how to best make the process your own. The following case study will help you to put the design thinking process – specifically empathy mapping – into perspective.

Use case – better course design through design thinking

A few years ago, I had a small business client who was selling their courses online in an asynchronous eLearning format. The courses they were selling centered around a proprietary framework of sorts that the company had developed. I was called in as a learning consultant as they were not selling many courses and saw high attrition rates in them.

After gaining access to their **Learning Management System (LMS)** and reviewing the courses, several issues with their existing learning surfaced:

- The company was running asynchronous eLearning courses that the learner could enroll in at any time, yet they had discussion boards. The purpose of a discussion board is for learners to engage with each other; without a cohort of learners present at the same time, it was the luck of the draw whether learners interacted on the discussion board at all, much less were in the course at the same time!

- The course included exercises for the learner to submit, but no one was facilitating or checking their work!

- The course information hierarchy was poorly structured and confusing to navigate.

- The visual look and feel of the course were weak: there were no compelling graphics or learner software interactions, colors were not on-brand, and the fonts chosen did not set a mood for the course.

- Basic accessibility standards for color contrast, video closed captioning, and alt tags to describe images had not been implemented.

> **Think about it**
>
> After reading not even four chapters of this book, you already know more than the instructional designer who designed this company's existing courses did!

The owners of this company had many ideas about how to *fix* their courses so that they would sell better. I listened to the stakeholders in each meeting, took notes, and offered suggestions. But they were not understanding the *ghost learner effect* that their courses were perpetuating: the course design was asking for learner engagement that it couldn't deliver.

The client felt strongly about keeping the course's discussion boards and assignments, yet was unwilling to move to a *cohort model* where learners learn together at their own pace, over a given period. They didn't want to have to bother with *course runs* and managing that process. And I didn't want to redesign courses that would most likely end up with the same problem they already had: low learner engagement.

> **Pause and reflect**
>
> What problem was I solving in this case? The client engaged me to *fix* their existing courses and increase course sales. As learning designers, it's not our role to increase the sales of courses but rather to design and develop effective learning experiences. Working with smaller companies that are trying to get the *most bang for their buck* is often a challenge as a contract ID. Clients may ask you to solve unrelated problems, such as increasing their sales.
>
> In this case, I had to continually redirect the client toward what I was engaged for – the learning, not the sales and marketing problem. The relevant initial problem was, *How might we increase learner engagement in our existing online courses?*

We were at a standstill. Well, at least I was.

During our next meeting, I asked the owners of the company whether any of the learners who had previously taken the course were employees, friends, or family members. My goal was to access previous learners to talk with them about their learning experience. I wanted to put some learners back in their course and ask them to do a think-aloud as they navigated a course module. I wanted to observe how a few learners approached the course and what they said, thought, felt, and did.

> **Think about it**
>
> What phase of the design thinking process was I attempting to get to by making this request?

To my surprise, the owners responded that almost every employee in the 30-person company had taken the existing courses and that all employees still had access to their courses. Fortunately, the company was using a small enterprise LMS that was not very sophisticated; no one asked me to see which employees did and did not finish their courses!

I reached out to about 10 employees who worked across three distinct work functions. To my surprise, five of these employees were willing to reopen a course they took and talk with me about it. Watching them navigate (and skip through!) elements of the course was interesting: while I did not have a set list of questions to ask each learner (which, in hindsight, might have been helpful), I was able to ask each learner open-ended questions surrounding each of the five major course issues I had identified.

I engaged and observed these five learners take and talk through the course. They talked about what they thought of the course and shared their feelings. After I completed the interviews, I compiled my notes and created an **empathy map** to synthesize my findings. My findings looked like this:

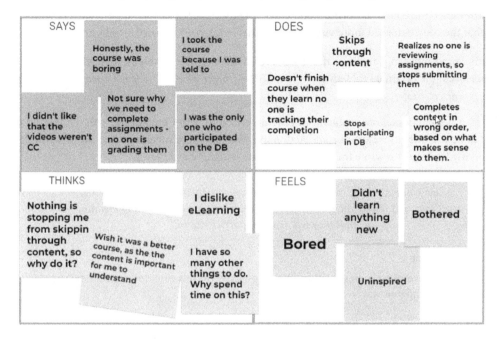

Figure 4.5 – A screenshot of the design thinking empathy map used for
a course redesign project, created in Google Jamboard

Here is a list of some of my *aha!* findings after completing this empathy map:

- The lack of course *learner controls* enabled learners to navigate to wherever they wanted, whenever they wanted – further confounding the issue of poorly structured information and low course completion rates.

> **Glossary**
>
> Learner controls, also known as **requirements**, necessitate that the learner must complete the requirement you define within a learning module (or lesson) before the module is marked complete. They can also prevent learners from moving on to the next module without completing the prior module first.

- Because learners were not required to complete anything, they took the course less seriously; they didn't find it meaningful.

- My hunches surrounding the assignments and discussion boards were spot on: learners actually *wanted* feedback and peer interaction – without it, they were not going to engage with these course components.

- They cited the course as boring – and when asked about this further, their answers confirmed that the course needed more visuals, and "better" videos with closed-captioning.

From my empathy map, I realized that I needed to reframe the problem. It needed to be more actionable than the original problem statement of *How might we increase learner engagement in our existing online courses?*

To design a better course, my problem statement needed to better empathize with the learners. It needed to be not only more specific and actionable but also more meaningful to my stakeholders. Based on my findings, I rewrote the project's problem statement as follows:

"How might we deliver learning that is well-organized, visually engaging, accessible, and makes the learner feel that they are part of something meaningful that they will want to participate in?"

> **Pause and reflect**
> Flex your creative muscle: based on my findings, can you reframe the client's new problem statement in a *different* way?

In my next meeting with the company owners, I shared my interview notes, empathy map, and revised problem statement. My stakeholders seemed surprised that their employees had been so honest – and, frankly, critical – of the courses. However, at the same time, they also seemed to appreciate my efforts and the feedback.

In the end, the client still did not want to change to a facilitator-guided cohort model for their eLearning. However, based on my empathy map and new problem statement, they were willing to accept suggestions to improve visual interest and graphics, refine videos with closed captioning, and improve the course's information hierarchy, which we implemented.

Since the client was unwilling to change to a cohort learning model, I suggested deleting the "ghost" discussion boards and assignments and, instead, created a downloadable self-reflective packet that learners could complete and then share with their team during upcoming departmental meetings. Since most of the existing courses were being purchased from my client by various organizations for their employees, this hybrid approach seemed like a good compromise. The hybrid solution would motivate each learner to complete their work, as they knew they would be tasked with sharing it. Moreover, by sharing their work, the need for peer interaction and feedback would be addressed.

In this case, my original solution was not accepted – something that every instructional designer will face when tasked with creative problem-solving. But by completing design thinking-style end user interviews and synthesizing user feedback into an empathy map, I was able to develop a more refined problem statement. This enabled me to move forward with a creative solution that was accepted by all, and while it wasn't perfect, the client seemed happy in the end. I completed the project with my confidence intact, knowing that future learners would be more motivated and engaged in their learning with the new course design.

Think about it

Using all of the information presented, can you brainstorm **3–5 other ways** this client's courses could have been redesigned?

Build your creative competency

Congratulations on (almost) completing this chapter on **The Creative Competency**. I hope this chapter has helped you realize that while most people are not born creative geniuses, we can indeed build our creative muscles.

It's time to provide a few additional resources to help build your creative competency. Again, this is a smorgasbord of resources: take what you want, leave what you don't.

Learn more about your own creative potential

Let's break the mold of what you previously thought about your creativity. These quick assessments are science based and will help to point you in the direction of what your creative strengths might be – as well as where your creativity could be developed.

Take a quick creativity assessment

The following statements describe the traits of creative individuals and were developed by Mihaly Csikszentmihalyi, the author of the best-selling book on creativity, *Flow*.

Assess your creativity by reading each statement. Which statements apply to you?

- Creative individuals have a great deal of energy, but they are also often quiet and at rest.

  Is this you? Yes __ No __

- Creative individuals tend to be smart, yet also naive at the same time.

  Is this you? Yes __ No __

- Creative individuals have a combination of playfulness and discipline, or responsibility and irresponsibility.

  Is this you? Yes __ No __

- Creative individuals alternate between imagination and fantasy at one end and a rooted sense of reality at the other.

  Is this you? Yes __ No __

- Creative people seem to harbor opposite tendencies on the continuum between extroversion and introversion.

  Is this you? Yes __ No __

- Creative individuals are also remarkably humble and proud at the same time.

  Is this you? Yes __ No __

- Creative individuals, to a certain extent, escape rigid gender role stereotyping and tend toward androgyny.

  Is this you? Yes __ No __

- Generally, creative people are thought to be rebellious and independent.

  Is this you? Yes __ No __

- Most creative people are passionate about their work, yet they can be extremely objective about it as well.

  Is this you? Yes __ No __

- The openness and sensitivity of creative individuals often expose them to suffering and pain yet also a great deal of enjoyment.

  Is this you? Yes __ No __

Source: *Creativity – Flow and the Psychology of Discovery and Invention* by Mihaly Csikszentmihalyi, 2013, fourth edition, pp. 58–73.

The more "Yes" answers you provided, the higher your innate creativity is, according to Csikszentmihalyi's creativity scale

Just for fun (and comparison's sake), now take the following creativity assessment, which was developed by researchers at the Kellogg School of Management at Northwestern University. This assessment will help you to decide whether you have the attitudes, personality traits, values, motivations, and interests that often characterize a creative individual. The assessment is based on years of study of the attributes had by people who work in fields in which creative thinking are common and it can be found at `https://www.kellogg.northwestern.edu/faculty/uzzi/ftp/page176.html`.

Continue to build your creativity with a growth mindset

If you feel like flexing your creative muscle immediately, check out these three easy exercises for practicing your creativity from Hokanson's text, *Developing Creative Thinking Skills: An Introduction for Learners*. They are so easy, you could even do them daily:

- **Exercise #1 – Build your openness to new experiences: Do, eat, and wear something different**

  This is a simple exercise to get you to practice being more open to new experiences. For example, one day *do* something different such as driving home a new way, the next day *eat* something new, and the next *wear* something different. Try a new *Do, eat, or wear* each day for a few months.

  These *Differents* don't need to be large changes, just small things that you can do to get yourself out of your ordinary rut and (perhaps) out of some undesirable habits. How can you create something different to become more open to new experiences? Vary your life experiences in a small way (at least to start) to increase your tolerance for different foods, clothes, places, and things. This will slowly help you to open your mind to new experiences.

- **Exercise #2 – Build your idea generation skills: 10 different uses for ordinary objects**

  You can complete this exercise while you're doing something mundane yet necessary, such as brushing your teeth. Find something in the bathroom (or wherever you are) and try to come up with *10 different uses* for that everyday object. For example, what could you use a bathroom towel for instead of just drying yourself off? Creative problem-solving is based on idea generation; practicing coming up with lots of *use* ideas for a simple object is a terrific way to practice this.

- **Exercise #3 – Preserve your most creative thoughts: Record your "AHA!" ideas**

  Research has shown that people often have more creative ideas when they're relaxed – and not really doing anything. You might hear about people having their most creative thoughts right when they wake up or maybe while they are showering. These are the types of ideas that we often lose or forget as the day goes on.

  Write things down to record these thoughts (or record them on your phone). The point is to record your ideas before you forget them. I have a co-worker who does this. She's always the one who people turn to for new ideas, not surprisingly.

Develop your comfort with ambiguity

As an instructional designer, you'll often find yourself in flux – and *not* in control. Being a designer means being in a state of change – and often anxiety-provoking ambiguity. Read more in this article from IDEO's blog on how to combat ambiguity anxiety: `https://www.ideo.com/blog/3-ways-to-get-comfortable-with-ambiguity`.

Appreciate the aesthetic design (and psychology) of everyday things

Learn about the connection between the needs of users, cognitive psychology, and product design in the epic read, *The Design of Everyday Things*. This article was written by cognitive scientist and founder of the NNG group, Don Norman.

Then, read Norman's follow-up book, *Emotional Design: Why we love or hate everyday things*, to learn how human psychology and emotions apply to the invention and design of new technologies and products – by addressing our feelings, reactions, and self-identities.

Learn the basics of UX/UI principles: join the **Interactive Design Foundation** (**IDF**). The IDF is a nonprofit organization dedicated to education in the field of UX/UI design. It's inexpensive and offers a multitude of next-to-free courses on HCI, UX/UI Design, accessibility, design thinking, augmented and virtual reality design, and more. Not to mention, it's a treasure trove of articles and information.

Here are a few links to get you familiarized with this wonderful educational organization:

- `https://www.interaction-design.org/`
- `https://www.interaction-design.org/literature/article/the-building-blocks-of-visual-design`
- `(https://www.interaction-design.org/literature/topics/ux-design)`.
- `(https://www.interaction-design.org/literature/topics/human-computer-interaction)`

Learn more about typography

Learn why the curation of the style, arrangement, and appearance of the letters, numbers, and symbols is so important, and how it sets the mood for digital experiences in these articles:

- **Typography Elements Everyone Needs to Understand**: `https://medium.com/gravitdesigner/typography-elements-everyone-needs-to-understand-5fdea82f470d#`
- **CreativeBits**: `https://creativebits.org/graphic-design/typography-101/`

Improve your learning designs' inclusivity with Universal Design for Learning (UDL)

Learn more about UDL and how this framework for course design optimizes learning for everybody. Then, download and save the CAST UDL graphic organizer to challenge your creativity in designing courses that improve learning for all. I have this job aid hanging on my office wall. It's a helpful tool for reminding me to provide multiple means of engagement, representation, and action/expression in my course design:

- `https://www.cast.org/impact/universal-design-for-learning-udl`
- `https://udlguidelines.cast.org/binaries/content/assets/udlguidelines/udlg-v2-2/udlg_graphicorganizer_v2-2_numbers-yes.pdf`

According to the Centers for Disease Control and Prevention, *up to 20% of learners in the US have a disability of some sort.* Learn more about the various types of disabilities and push your course design creativity by making your digital learning experiences to be even more inclusive:

- `https://elearningindustry.com/elearning-accessibility-best-practices-tips-tricks`
- `https://www.cdc.gov/ncbddd/disabilityandhealth/infographic-disability-impacts-all.html`
- `https://webaim.org/resources/contrastchecker`

Learn more about the creative process from these experts

If you've ever wondered how people are motivated – and the relationship between motivation and creativity – Robert Franken's seminal text, **Human Motivation**, will be of interest.

Read more about how to become more creative in your ID practice in this article by creativity professors and researchers Gregory Clinton and Brad Hokanson – and how they layered creative problem-solving onto instructional design's ADDIE model: `https://www.semanticscholar.org/paper/Creativity-in-the-training-and-practice-of-the-Clinton-Hokanson/596038ad8786b16063eb254ea9139fc5e6372f1e`.

Are you still doubtful that creativity can be learned? To learn more, listen to this National Public Radio podcast, *Creativity, Learned, or Innate?*, featuring Dr. Nancy Andreasen, American neuroscientist /neuropsychiatrist and the Andrew H. Woods Chair of Psychiatry at the Roy J. and Lucille A. Carver College of Medicine at the University of Iowa: `https://www.npr.org/transcripts/6631146?storyId=6631146&ft=nprml&f=6631146`.

Take a deep dive into design thinking and creative problem-solving

There are many takes and variations on design thinking. What I consider to be the most valuable is the original method, developed by David and Tom Kelley of IDEO and founders of the **Stanford d.school**. This entirely complete, well-written guide will answer all of your questions on the design thinking method and can be found at `https://web.stanford.edu/~mshanks/MichaelShanks/files/509554.pdf`.

A MUST read for those who look to build their creative problem-solving and design thinking skills, and written by IDEO partners David and Tom Kelley, *Creative Confidence* is an easy read with many practical tips and exercises for how to effectively use design thinking and develop your creative problem-solving skills. It can be found at `https://www.creativeconfidence.com/`.

Learn more about the empathy phase of human-centered design by digging deeper into empathy mapping, complete with step-by-step instructions, by going to `https://www.ideo.com/blog/build-your-creative-confidence-empathy-maps`.

Summary

This chapter highlighting **The Creativity Competency** in instructional design has, hopefully, opened your eyes to the different meanings of creativity, and how they intersect in the field of learning design. Learning how to think like a designer – because you ARE a designer – will help you to design and develop more innovative and useful solutions for your learners, team, stakeholders, and/or clients.

If you haven't had much artistic design experience, my hope is that this chapter has opened your eyes to the different types of creativity and how to develop and strengthen your instructional design *practice*. Even if you've never heard of the concepts discussed in this chapter, you'll now be able to truly creatively problem-solve like a designer.

In our next and final chapter, we'll discuss the importance of being able to **effectively communicate** your (fabulously) creative ideas and solutions to all stakeholders and, most importantly, win their buy-in.

Project Communication in Instructional Design

"As a client, I try to put myself in the shoes of the ID and judge whether I have given them enough clear information and briefing to deliver what I need. Having a vision in my head isn't good enough. For IDs, I would encourage them to get into the head of the client very early in the process!"

– Jo Davey – Head of Learning, GroupM

Effective communication and collaboration in instructional design can be compared to the steps we take when we follow a recipe. We might have all the ingredients that are needed, but without communicating the steps, the recipe can't be finished. As instructional designers, it's our role to ensure transparent communication of the steps needed to complete a given instructional design project.

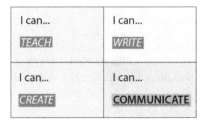

Figure 5.1 – The Four Competencies Model

In this chapter, we'll review:

- What effective communication and collaboration mean in instructional design
- How to communicate throughout the ADDIE instructional design process through an *agile* lens
- A real-world use case highlighting the importance of communication in the early stages of the ADDIE model or **Successive Approximation Model (SAM)**
- Resources to help you to instill effective communication and collaboration into any ID project

Effective communication and collaboration in instructional design

Here, we will use the ADDIE model to discuss best practices for communicating before, during, and after your instructional design projects. This means transparent communication coming both from you, the ID, and from others – such as stakeholders, **subject matter experts (SMEs)**, and any relevant cross-functional team members – throughout the ADDIE process. As instructional design projects often involve multiple stakeholders, the need for effective communication in this field is high. If communication (and therefore collaboration) falls short, your project may not only be delayed but, also be at risk of not meeting its intended learning and performance goals.

The forms of communication you use to collaborate throughout an instructional design project may vary. For example, it may be verbal and done in person or via phone or virtual meetings – or written, via in-file comments, messaging tools such as Slack™, shared project management tools, or email. Whichever form of communication you are using, setting expectations for what you see as the *desired* form and cadence of communication at the outset of each project is *key*.

Before we dive into communication and collaboration throughout the ADDIE model, let's answer the question: what *is* effective collaboration and communication in instructional design? In their research paper, *Instructional Designer Competencies: American and European Comparisons*, Koszalka et al. (https://bit.ly/3JbqJGN) cite nine communications-based competencies for IDs:

- Deliver written communications (emails, messages, in-file comments) that are grammatically correct, actionable, and clear

- Present project information that communicates project needs and accomplishments

- Listen actively

- Ask for, provide, and address constructive feedback

- Send written and oral messages that take into account the type of audience being communicated to (for example, SME, cross-functional team member, stakeholder, learner)

- Collaborate and build consensus effectively

- Negotiate and resolve conflict diplomatically

- Use questioning techniques to be able to effectively address project needs and stakeholder concerns

- Share your project's status via summary updates

As you can see, effective collaboration and communication in instructional designer involves being part project manager, part salesperson, and even part mediator. With time (and hopefully with some of what you learn in this chapter), you'll be able to manage your projects' timelines and stakeholders and successfully advocate for your ideas. You'll be able to communicate and collaborate effectively on all of your ID projects, regardless of the barriers.

Agile communication throughout the ADDIE model

As we discussed in *Chapter 2, The Teaching Competency*, ADDIE continues to be the longest tenure and most popular model for the instructional design process. Even if the organization you are working with does not 100% follow the full ADDIE model, you can still use the phases of ADDIE as the basis for how you communicate and collaborate on a given ID project.

The ability to manage your project by being nimble and agile in the way you iterate your learning project is the key to meeting your deliverables' timelines. While we will look at the ADDIE model in this chapter, we'll examine it through the lens of an *iterative lifecycle*, versus a *one-and-done* linear process.

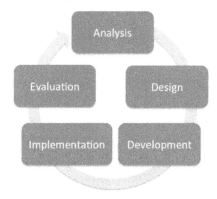

Figure 5.2 – A review of ADDIE (by Dave Braunschweig – Own work, CC BY-SA
3.0, https://commons.wikimedia.org/w/index.php?curid=31359973)

While other instructional design models are, by nature, more agile, such as the **Successive Approximation Model (SAM)** (https://mylearning.nps.gov/agile-instructional-design/), which incorporates a continual loop of analysis, designing, and development, it does not talk about *project implementation* or *a separate evaluation phase*. As such, we'll stick with the ADDIE model – but through the lens of how *agile communication and collaboration* techniques can be applied to each stage of ADDIE.

The following diagram shows how the ADDIE model might also be agile:

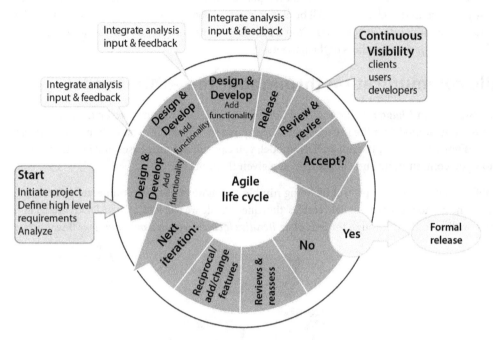

Figure 5.3 – ADDIE as an agile life cycle adopted from Unger and Novak (2011), courtesy of Dianne Rees, https://instructionaldesignfusions.wordpress.com/2012/09/29/agile-instructional-design/

Now that you know that ADDIE can be approached through an agile and iterative lens, let's take a deep dive into how this can be applied to improve project communications in each stage of ADDIE.

The analysis phase – best practices for kicking off your project

How you start your project in the analysis phase is the most important indicator of your project's success. Think of the analysis phase as getting off on the right foot. You're essentially setting expectations for your project's form, amount, frequency, and nature of communication.

The best way to do this is to have a formal **project kick-off meeting**. In the agile world of software development, this type of kick-off meeting is usually referred to as the *savvy start* meeting. The idea of having this more formal starting-the-project meeting can be tricky – especially if you are working with a small team or a single stakeholder. People may think they don't need such a meeting, *but you do*.

This initial meeting is important for many reasons. First, it establishes the who's who on the project and enforces teamwork and timelines. It also answers many questions for those who are involved and gives all team members the forum to ask further questions that pertain to their specific roles in the project. The kick-off meeting is also a wonderful way to communicate and get *buy-in* on agreed-upon collaboration expectations for the project. Lastly, it serves as a source of truth to refer to if the project happens to go off track.

A kick-off meeting should be attended by the instructional design team, the PM (if one has been assigned), all internal or external stakeholders, and, if possible, cross-functional teams or services, such as art directors, graphic designers, or video production personnel.

If the learning project involves particularly technical or dense material, you may also want to involve at least one potential or already-assigned SME. Often, the PM will facilitate the kick-off meeting; however, if you're working in a smaller organization, chances are you may not have one. In that case, the lead instructional designer should facilitate the meeting.

> **Think about it**
>
> Whether they're internal or external, *your stakeholders are your clients*. You are designing to meet their learning needs. People may not think they need to spend time clarifying a project that seems straightforward. Don't fall into the trap of not getting early stakeholder buy-in by skipping the kick-off meeting.

The content and duration of your meeting may vary, depending on how far along you may (or may not) have progressed with identifying the learning problem at hand and its potential solutions. I like to keep my kick-off meetings to 45 minutes, as this time frame forces me to be extra organized for my part of the meeting.

If the learning experience's delivery modality has already been agreed upon, and the learning and performance goals have already been set, then your meeting may be shorter. It's important to note that *all earlier decisions* should be recapped in the project brief of the kick-off meeting for the benefit of any stakeholder who may have joined the project later.

Items to discuss in a kick-off meeting

What you cover in a kick-off meeting can also vary a bit, depending on whether you are working with an external client or you're holding it for your internal team. There are many commonalities between both scenarios – as an ID project is, in the end, an ID project – no matter who you're designing for. In the meetings I've held and attended, after introductions are made, there are usually five agenda items that should be covered during a kick-off meeting.

Agenda item one – team introductions and the project brief

After quick team introductions, the first thing you'll need to share is what your general scope of work is, or a project brief. While the following content may seem like a lot to include at the beginning of your kick-off meeting, you can easily visually present the project brief in the first slide or two of your meeting's presentation deck.

Your project brief slide(s) should contain the following:

- **The project summary**: For example "We create two asynchronous eLearning courses for *how to give feedback* and *how to receive feedback that addresses the input we received from our most recent employee listening survey for more training.* The learning modules will include one leader video in each course, learner content interactions, scenario assessments, and one job aid for each course."

- **The desired performance outcome**: For example, "managers will learn the principles and best practices for giving and receiving feedback".

- **An explanation of the learner's experience in these courses**: "Learners will start each course by watching a leader video on the importance of giving or receiving feedback effectively. They will then read content and complete different interactions to learn about our approach to feedback. Lastly, they will complete a scenario between two people – one receiving and one giving feedback – and be able to download a job aid with the best practices highlighted for their quick reference".

- **The target learner audience**: A target audience for this example project might be "all managers, levels III-VI."

- **The development tools and LMS you will be using**: For example, Articulate Rise™, Storyline™, or a virtual instructor-led training PowerPoint, and the LMS platform that will host the course.

- **The desired duration for each course**: For example, 30 minutes.

- **The metrics or measurements**: Think about KPIs or any other specific metrics this organization wants to measure.

- **The key stakeholders**: What department (or company) are you creating this project for and who are your main contacts? What is their organizational chain of command?

I strongly suggest presenting your project brief *visually*, not in long-form bullet-pointed paragraphs. Remember, you're incorporating the brief right into your kick-off deck, so you'll want it to be concise, using no more than one or two slides. For example, your visual project brief might look something like this:

Project Brief | How to give and receive feedback

Project Summary

Create two asynchronous eLearning courses for: 1) *How to give feedback* and 2) *How to receive feedback*
Each course will address managers' request for more training on giving/receiving FB. Each course will include one leader video and one downloadable job aid.

Target audience: Line managers levels III-VI. Global audience

Duration | tools: 20 min each; Rise

Measurement | KPI: Train 75% of all managers III-VI by EOY FY2023

Stakeholders: Jose Becerra, Vivian Lu

Desired Performance Outcomes

Managers will learn how to comfortably and effectively give and receive feedback.

Learner experience: Learners will take two, 20-minute *Articulate Rise* courses with leader video and content interactions. At the end of each course, they will complete a 'feedback scenario' to assess their new knowledge.

Content map: Feedback courses

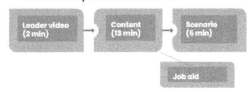

Figure 5.4 – Example of a visual project brief

Pause and reflect

If you can't answer most of the aforementioned points for your project brief slides, then you may not be ready for a kick-off meeting. If this is the case, you and your core team will need to revert to having a *strategy meeting* first.

If you can answer most of the project brief points – but still have a few outstanding items – no worries; this is what your kick-off meeting is for.

Agenda item two – learning design slides

This is your opportunity to get a lot of your questions out of the way for your upcoming project. As you show these slides, make sure you tell the team there will be a Q&A at the end of the meeting as well so that you can ensure all your questions are answered first. You don't need to let the team members in your kick-off meeting know you're about to barrage them with a series of questions.

Call these slides *Learning design* and just start asking! The following questions represent ideas for the types of answers you might need to properly kick off your project. Remember, the following questions are just a guide. Depending on your project type, you may need to ask more or less of these general ID questions:

- **Are there specific branding/look and feel guidelines that we need to adhere to?** In the case of an external client, if you don't already have their brand guidelines, ask for them now (colors, fonts, and other imagery and design conventions).

- **What type of accessibility should be included in this learning experience?** For example, do your stakeholders want video close captioning and transcript downloads? Are they firmly against drag-and-drops interactions due to its inaccessibility to some learners? To what extent do they want visual accessibility standards enforced – for example, image alt tags, color contrast, heading conventions, and so on? Is there anything else they are looking for in this area?

- **Will there be additional reviewers for this project?** For example, any SMEs? If so, how many? Remember, the SME review should happen in the earliest stages of the design process, so ask these questions now.

- **What kind of assessment would you like to incorporate into the course?** Will there be quizzes or culminative exams or alternate assessment forms such as self-reflection?

- **Are there any other cross-functional team members/stakeholders that will be involved in the project?** Make sure to ask about potential outside contributors who may not be present at the meeting, such as in-house video production or graphic design.

- **What is the tone and "voice" of this project?** Is it formal, professional, or conversational? Are there specific writing conventions you'd like to follow, such as sentence case for headings, the Oxford comma, or other organizational guidelines?

- **Are you familiar with the "alpha," "beta," and "gold" aspects of course development?** Asking this question is always a good idea. It gives you a chance to ascertain your stakeholders' experience with previous learning design projects and allows you to review the three phases and iterations of an eLearning development project. It also sneaks in expectations surrounding team review cycles. A suggested recap might go something like this:

  - "First we will create a design document or storyboard for you to review and add your comments to before we start the actual eLearning prototype development process. All SMEs and stakeholders will weigh in during this process." Then, move on by explaining the prototyping process, or *Alpha, Beta, Gold*.

    - **Alpha**: This is the first course proto, during which content, interactions, slight structural elements, and images are reviewed and changed. All stakeholders should weigh in during this phase.

    - **Beta**: This is the prototype and shows all of the requested changes to be made to the alpha. This review includes making sure all changes were captured, and a review for smaller errors and inconsistencies such as punctuation, grammar, typos, and minor image changes. Large change requests are not addressed at beta. Key stakeholders weigh in during this phase.

    - **Gold**: This is the final iteration. The course is ready to launch – most likely to a small group of pilot learners to get feedback and iterate based on the pilot group's feedback before the organization brings the learning experience to scale.

- **How will the course be launched in the Learning Managment System (LMS)?** For example, SCORM 1.2, xAPI, or another way (see the *Building your project communications competency* section of this chapter for more information on these course implementation methods).

- **What kind of evaluation procedures might be put into place?** While it may be early on in the project to approach this topic, remind the team that evaluation is part of the *iterative and continuous improvement* ID cycle. It's best to ascertain whether the team is looking for pre-course evaluations, during-course evaluation, and what types of post-course evaluation they may be looking for now.

Agenda item three – the project timeline and program management tool

After you address any client or stakeholder questions, your next slide will show a (very) high-level project timeline. If you have a **PM** facilitating the meeting, the timeline and duration of the project should be explained by them; if not, the ID will present the timeline. For this slide, I suggest first showing only project milestones to give the big picture – a 10,000-foot view of the project:

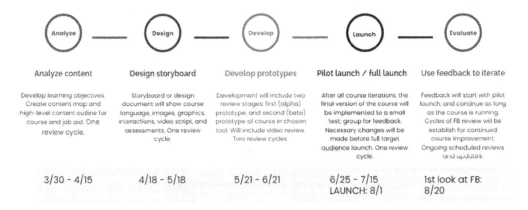

Figure 5.5 – High-level project timeline

During the project timeline conversation, you'll explain the next phases of the project – content analysis and design, and what to expect during the first stakeholder and SME review of the course design document and possibly storyboard. You will then explain the development phase and the prototype review process (again) in the eLearning authoring tool.

Sharing your project management tool

You've taken a big step toward running a more streamlined, agile, and less siloed ID project by having this kick-off meeting – and getting all relevant stakeholders' buy-in. Now, you must introduce the project management tool that will be used during the project (see the *Building your project communications competency* section of this chapter for more information on PM tools in ID).

You've shown the kick-off meeting attendees the big-picture milestone timeline. Now, embed a link to your digital tool here, and give the meeting attendees a quick overview of the milestones and task-level view, explaining the review points and task owners as you go along. At the end of this overview, share the PM tool with all participants, if you haven't done so already. The following screenshot shows an example of a project timeline using the PM tool Asana:

Figure 5.6 – Example of an ID project in a digital PM tool (Asana)

I like to chunk out the project tasks as much as possible in the PM tool – especially for more complicated course development. I find that chunking helps to stop little problems from getting big. For example, if you're developing a longer, 10-12 lesson eLearning experience, you might want to get a prototype review for two to three lessons at a time.

By chunking out your development and incorporating as many review checkpoints as possible into your project, you'll enable all team members to *spot problems early on* and minimize major revisions. Your project will move along more quickly – and you'll be able to finish faster and without those dreaded late-in-the-game major revision requests.

> **Think about it**
>
> I once consulted for a Fortune 100 company that used Excel as their PM tool. While these spreadsheets lived on the firm's SharePoint site and therefore were live files, only the PM could mark off what tasks had been completed by the team.
>
> The result? No one ever looked at the team's project plans – except for the PM! Project management tools such as Asana™, Basecamp™ – and yes, even Excel on a SharePoint site – are meant to be collaboration tools. Allow each team member to own their tasks – and mark off their status. By doing this, you are encouraging not only team collaboration, but also *ownership*.

Agenda item four – stakeholder questions

You will want to set aside 5-10 minutes of meeting time for your stakeholders' follow-up questions, as they may need more clarification on certain points discussed – or have different ideas about how to move the project forward. Hopefully, by already providing a project brief and discussing the project's timeline and review processes, your stakeholders will not have many questions.

However, always make sure you spend adequate time here by pausing and asking for questions and input to ensure the highest level of project collaboration and buy-in. Push-back from stakeholders is always easier to deal with early rather than later on in the project.

Agenda item five – follow-up action items

Lastly, you will want to create a final slide for action items/to-dos. These should be categorized for the following:

- Stakeholders
- Instructional designers
- The PM (if applicable)

To-do action items might be to forward additional source material, provide learning goals or objectives, or furnish SME names and titles. Always include a due date and type in these to-dos during the meeting to increase team accountability.

Someone should be taking notes throughout the kick-off meeting, preferably right into the PowerPoint presentation. Your meeting will be held virtually.

If your meeting is held virtually, you may want to also ask someone to record the meeting. Then, embed the kick-off meeting's PowerPoint deck and meeting recording directly into your PM tool for team members' future reference.

Starting your content analysis

With your kick-off meeting under your belt and necessary stakeholder source information delivered, you're ready to start your project's content analysis. If learning objectives have not yet been set, creating your course's learning objectives and delivering a high-level content outline will be your next steps after the kick-off meeting.

While the course learning objectives you share with stakeholders should be precise and reflect the learning and performance goals stated in the project brief, the high-level course outline need not be as detailed. At this point, you are simply setting the overall structure of the course.

For the most part, I structure each course lesson/section so that it correlates with each learning objective. You may want to offer just the course learning objectives and a high-level content map with some follow-up bullet points showing the subjects and principles you intend to cover.

The idea here is to not overwhelm your stakeholders right out of the gate. Remember, some organizations' stakeholders will labor over the *perfect* wording of learning objectives (for example, in higher education), while others are not as picky about the wording if they think the objectives will ultimately guide the desired behavior change. Getting your stakeholders' buy-in on the overall structure of the course and specific learning objectives at this point will prevent dissent later down the road.

With the transparent communication you incorporated in your kick-off meeting and the collaboration on your learning goals and the course's overall structure, you're now ready to move to the design phase of ADDIE.

The design phase – keeping comments and collaboration on track

The design phase is where you will create a more detailed design document, and if you're using a more customized authoring tool such as Articulate Storyline™, possibly a storyboard. Your goal is to address content and structural change requests here – *not* in development. As such, it's a key phase of your project for communication and collaboration.

Many IDs will skip the design document or storyboard phase and go right into development – especially if they are responsible for both course design and development. This approach can be a bit of a slippery slope, as many stakeholders (especially SMEs) prefer reviewing content initially via a written script/design document.

Of course, there are some instances where it is plausible that you may forge ahead into development without first creating a design document or storyboard. This might happen if you're designing a short, straightforward course for microlearning for stakeholders that you've already designed for and know, and/or are developing in a less customized software tool such as Articulate Rise™.

There are a few more reasons not to skip the design document: despite the powerful course prototype review tools available in eLearning authoring tools (such as Articulate 360 Review™), remember that there will always be stakeholders who prefer reviewing content in a Word document instead of a prototype. Lastly, for some IDs, laying out the design document helps to further hone their thoughts surrounding course language, graphics, and key learner interactions.

> ### A note about SME reviews
>
> The **Subject Matter Expert (SME)** review should take place early, at the course outline or the design document of the review. SMEs are often busy people with little time. As such, it's best to give them as much pure content as you can, without a lot of proposed graphics and interaction noise.
>
> One approach a large technology client took was cutting and pasting the content of all the project's design documents into one giant, separate file just so the SMEs would *only* see the content. The thought here was to keep the SME reviews on track by only providing the content.

Provide the design document or storyboard to your stakeholders and SMEs *as soon as you can* after your kick-off meeting. People are busy and memories are short. It's best to provide it within a week or two of your kick-off meeting to keep your project's momentum going.

In your written communications surrounding the delivery of the design document, you will want to communicate best collaboration practices to your stakeholders and SMEs for review of these files. For example, for the comments that the team leaves, *how will each comment be resolved and closed?*

I've worked with agile organizations that allow the ID to resolve, comment back, and close out each reviewer's comments. I have also worked with organizations that dictate that only each reviewer can close out/resolve their comments. The latter method can be quite vexing if your stakeholders/reviewers are traveling, in all-day meetings, or simply forget to circle back to close out/resolve their comments after you've addressed the issue.

Being able to address and resolve/close out your reviewers' comments (at least the low-hanging fruit, such as typos) is by far the most efficient and effective approach – and gives you more control over the review process. If possible, set expectations with your stakeholders for this type of collaborative review process *before* they start their reviews in the email that houses the design document or storyboard link.

More on stakeholder comments

Whether we're talking about stakeholder review comments left in a design document file or an alpha proto Articulate 360 Review™ file, most reviewer feedback is genuinely constructive. However, curt and condescending comments can and do happen.

As an instructional designer, it's important to leave your ego at the door. Don't take these types of non-constructive feedback personally. Often, reviewers are busy with other work priorities and are moving through their reviews on your learning project at lightning speed; they may not even realize they're being rude!

When you read a comment that makes you react emotionally, *don't respond to it immediately.* Check through for the easier questions first, address those, then circle back to that stickier feedback. You'll be glad you did.

After your design document or storyboard has been vetted by all stakeholders and SMEs, and comments and iterations have been resolved, it's time to move your course to the next ADDIE phase: communication and collaboration in development.

The development phase – guiding your prototype reviews

In larger organizations or on the eLearning agency side, instructional design is often parceled out by the ADDIE phase. In some organizations, those at the analysis and design phases are called learning designers or learning experience designers (not IDs), while those who *develop* eLearning courses are called instructional designers or developers. In smaller organizations or consultancies, learning designers/IDs might work throughout the entire ID process, from analysis to evaluation.

Whatever your organization's situation is, the development of your prototype must be reviewed by your stakeholders, and the process may vary based on whether development is being done by you or by a separate development team. Whichever the development process, I recommend chunking-out portions of your prototypes to your reviewers instead of giving stakeholders an entire 60-minute learning experience to review. This can work wonders for speeding up your prototype reviews, especially at the alpha phase.

In my contracts, I explicitly state that there are two review rounds for the design phase and two reviews for the development phase. If I'm on a simpler project and have not created a design document or storyboard for an Articulate Rise™ course, the two review rounds policy in the prototype development phase still applies.

I've learned the hard way to be extremely specific when sending out software review links. I now have a couple of emails saved that I cut and paste from that recap what *can and cannot be reviewed* during both the alpha and beta phases. I have also learned to include specific *review-by* dates in both my alpha and beta review request emails.

The alpha prototype review

This should be an all-stakeholder review after the initial alpha prototype course has been built. It includes a review for minor structure issues, content, clarity, sources/context, functionality, branding, and typos/grammar. Christy Tucker (`https://www.christytuckerlearning.com/`), an ID not only known for her exemplary work, but also for her project management prowess, suggests the following items to be included in emailed requests for reviews:

- Your email to the reviewers should include the alpha course *review link* and what you perceive to be important during the alpha review phase – for example, "as you review, note that minor content structure, content deletions, and minor content add requests can be addressed (such as sources). Please also review this prototype course for functionality (does everything work?), branding inconsistencies, and typo/grammatical errors".

- If you have anything that you are forwarding that is under construction, such as key video or graphic development, make sure you call these out as such in your email as well so that your reviewers don't comment on items that have not yet been completed.

The beta prototype review

The beta review should only be done by key stakeholders. It includes a review of course functionality, typos/grammatical errors, and branding inconsistencies. For beta review communications, Tucker recommends including the following:

- Your email to reviewers should include the beta course *review link,* when you would like the course to be reviewed (in the subject line and body of the email), and indicate what you perceive to be important during the beta review phase – for example, as you review, look for any functionality issues (does everything work?), minor branding inconsistencies, and any possible typos.

- It's also important to emphasize that this is a *final* review and that no structural or content changes will be made.

> **Remember**
>
> Allowing major changes during the beta review process will not only prevent you from delivering your project on time, but also cause extra work (and worry) on your behalf. You have done your due diligence in communicating the timeline and review processes. Someone else's change of heart or emergency is not *your* emergency.

Depending on the organization, I will usually wait until all stakeholder reviews are completed before I pop back into the software to make the requested changes. By waiting until I've received all comments, I'm able to make changes ideally only once versus several times.

This method usually works for most organizations. However, in some organizations that are hyper-agile in their approach, iterating as your review comments come in is a common practice. This approach saves time, especially if it's known that certain stakeholders will not be able to get to their review during your requested time frame.

> **Think about it**
>
> There will always be disorganized, apathetic, or sometimes even incompetent reviewers in every organization. By stating the number of reviews, they get it up front – even in your kick-off meeting – and know what they should look for and do during each review phase. By clearly stating or expectations upfront (and repeating them through the design and development phases), you'll curb late reviews or random stakeholders jumping in at the beta phase suggesting last-minute course content changes.

The implementation phase – your product's launch

Think of a learning experience's implementation stage as the where, when, and how of your course. Implementation marks the first time that true learners will interact with your course. It's showtime!

However, as obviously important as implementation is, many instructional designers may not be a part of the implementation process. To a certain extent, an ID's involvement in the implementation stage will vary based on whether they are a contractor (who may not have access to the LMS or other tools needed for the course's launch), or whether the ID is internal to the organization.

Just because an ID is internal to an organization, however, doesn't mean that they'll be involved with the implementation of a course they designed. For instance, many organizations see the actual implementation of an eLearning course not as the domain of instructional design, but rather as that of other departments, such as the learning implementation department or even the general IT department. Furthermore, IDs are often more than happy to complete a course and give it to someone else to implement.

If the organization you're working with has adopted a **phased approach** to their learning, the ID will often become at least partly involved in the implementation. For example, the ID might provide getting started or *pre-learning* event materials to improve comprehension of future course content.

These types of phased learning materials might come in the way of pre-learning surveys, pre-course primer content, or even training the trainer if the experience is live or a **Virtual Instructor-Led Training (VILT)** course. In all phased pre-learning cases, the ID will need to be aware of the course launch timelines, how and where it will be launched, and any pilot launches.

About train-the-trainer

If you're tasked with training the trainer after designing a learning experience to implement/launch an in-person or synchronous VILT, make sure you impart the following in addition to the PowerPoint deck you created:

- The course's overall employee performance/behavior change goal
- Its learning objectives
- An explanation of the course's activities (for example, partner work or break-out rooms) and why they were designed
- An explanation of interactions such as in-course surveys or whiteboard usage and why they were designed
- Any assessments, and how to best deliver them

> **Remember**
> The learning experience you design is only as successful as its implementation!

Another benefit to being in the loop of the implementation process is to be available to answer/address any functionality issues that might not have been caught during the development process. It's often the first users who may circle back to the stakeholders for whom the course was developed and share what they perceive to be issues with the learning experience. Being close to the course implementation allows the ID to iterate any glitches quickly and before the course is launched to more learners.

Lastly, being at least peripherally involved in the implementation process allows you to get early access to feedback surveys during a pilot launch – and to iterate the course as necessary before its full launch.

The evaluation phase – communicating your course's assessment plan

You've done it: the training has been launched, and the feedback is starting to come in. Evaluating your training is the last step in ADDIE – but certainly not the last step in your continued quality improvement efforts. Think of the feedback you receive as the impetus to learn, iterate, and improve everything you design. Evaluation is the *ultimate* form of effectively communicating and collaborating in instructional design.

Learning and development researcher Kurt Kraiger has identified three major reasons why instructional designers should evaluate the learning experiences they create:

- **Feedback**: Evaluating your courses provides feedback to IDs and instructors alike. This allows you to iterate and re-design the course and instructional efforts to be more engaging and effective.

- **Decision-making**: The information you glean from evaluations can inform the need for *future* courses or training programs. It also gives you information about instructors and the quality of the instruction in the case of in-person or VILT.

- **Marketing**: You can use the results of the data collected to demonstrate the value of your training to upper management, other key stakeholders, or future clients (if you're a contractor).

It's important to note that even though evaluation is listed as the last phase in the traditional linear ADDIE model, in the more agile ADDIE life cycle model, the evaluation phase loops right back into the analysis and (re)design. There are three touchpoints in which you can evaluate and iterate learning.

First, you may want to look for pre-learning experience feedback in the form of a **pre-survey** – in which you will assess a learner's knowledge and attitudes on the subject before instruction. Second, you can also evaluate learning during a learning experience through a **formative survey**.

Lastly, you can evaluate learning upon completion of a learning experience in a **summative survey** given after the course. Think of these three feedback touchpoints as the diagnosis (pre-survey), the check-up (formative survey), and the post-mortem after it's all done (summative survey).

Your evaluation communication plan

Collaborating and openly communicating with all stakeholders is especially important during survey development. By doing so, you'll reduce the potential for bias by getting a diverse array of points of view, which will help you to more objectively frame your course evaluation questions. Developing a reporting and communication plan to disseminate evaluation results will also help you to actively interact with your stakeholders during the evaluation process.

Your evaluation communication plan should include several components. First, you'll want to identify all stakeholders – and what they need to learn from this evaluation. Different stakeholders will have different values and needs for answers from this evaluation, so make sure that you include all stakeholders – and what you think they'd like to learn from the evaluation.

As you develop your course evaluation(s), try to incorporate all stakeholders' perspectives – and let them know you are doing so. Involve them in a shared document with survey questions to write and edit, and function as the editor of the feedback survey.

Next, as learners take the course and complete their summative evaluations, plan how to report the evaluation results to your stakeholders. Think about how you'll summarize the data in terms of different formats, both written and visual. Try to communicate your evaluation's results in a variety of formats that may appeal to your stakeholders.

You will also want to include different findings summaries based on each stakeholder's needs and purpose. For example, one stakeholder might be concerned about measuring the behavior change as related to the stated performance goal; another might be interested in measuring the potential long-term **Return on Investment (ROI)** of the course. Lastly, consider how you'll communicate the evaluation's results, whether it be a live presentation, an email, or a brief using data visualization tools and written content.

If you are a vendor working with a client, you may or may not be looped into the evaluation stage. Whether or not you design the survey instrument(s), you should always ask for course feedback to be sent to you for your professional growth and edification. This is obviously of foremost importance if you're still working with the client but even if you've parted ways, it's still a best practice to ask for feedback on the learning experiences you've designed for them – if they are willing to share it.

As you can see, communication is important throughout the ADDIE life cycle. As instructional designers, we tend to focus most of our communications efforts on the comments left by stakeholders during the design and development stages. As this chapter has presented, however, proactively communicating throughout the ADDIE process is just as important – especially in the early, kick-off stages of your project – to ensure an iterative and agile ID process.

I hope this section on how to foster agile communication and collaboration throughout the ADDIE life cycle has been helpful. Next, we will examine a real-world use case in which you'll see the impacts of skipping communication best practices in the initial stages of an ID project.

Use case: Don't skip the project setup meeting

This case study is about assumptions: the assumptions I made about a key stakeholder's knowledge of the instructional design process – and the steps I didn't take.

The client, a large multinational company, has several divisions. I had previously worked under contract with another division of this company with success, due in part to the key stakeholder's effective communication and collaboration efforts. In my previous project, this stakeholder was responsible for launching several learning initiatives to specific target audiences. They reviewed the context of each initiative and target learner audience with me and scheduled a regular cadence of meetings throughout the project.

As my contract with this client came to a close, they referred me to another division that was looking for an ID. I met with the new stakeholder and submitted a detailed proposal that was accepted within a few weeks. I was contracted to develop the learning objectives for several eLearning courses and then design and develop them.

Since I had previously worked with a division of the same company, I assumed that the cadence of communication and collaboration with this new stakeholder would be the same. As such, I did not fully set up the project at its outset.

Think about it

I assumed that one stakeholder would behave like another since they were part of the same greater organizational structure. This was indeed not the case.

What are some specific steps that I could have taken at the outset of this project?

During our initial meeting, the stakeholder offered a verbal project summary, including the performance goals and desired behavior change outcomes, the target learner audiences, and ideas surrounding the development tool (Articulate Rise™) and the LMS's capabilities. It seemed to be a complete verbal project briefing.

Even though I had not structured a formal kick-off deck or project timeline, I did ask the usual learning design and development questions, such as about brand and writing style guides, additional reviewers and stakeholders, course evaluation methods, the involvement of cross-functional team members, and the review process.

But then, slowly, the project started going off-track...

The first out-of-the-ordinary thing that happened was receiving an email with a video-only style course link. The stakeholder wanted to emulate this style for our courses – not quite possible in the chosen delivery tool, Articulate Rise 360™.

Later that week, I received another email from the stakeholder with a PDF from another course provider asking me to follow its design direction for the course's job aids. Sadly, this piece's design style contradicted the company's corporate brand guidelines.

Pause and reflect

These items were not part of our original discussion surrounding developing our courses. What should I have done?

Always ascertain what your stakeholder might want. In this case, I provided previous examples of Articulate Rise™ courses immediately to avoid confusion and disappointment with the chosen course delivery tool (we stuck with Rise). In the case of the job-aid design request, the graphic design was taken on by internal stakeholders.

Within a few weeks of working on the project, I had not received any source content for one of the courses, so I emailed the stakeholder to offer some content ideas and try to get the conversation going.

> **Think about it**
>
> No matter how good your research abilities are, you simply can't read your stakeholders' minds! Never move into design with less than baseline content.
>
> Don't allow important queries surrounding course content to go unanswered for long periods. During your next face-to-face or virtual meeting, force these important questions on to the stakeholder to at least get a verbal response. Then, as you piece together the course content, continuously check for the validity of your efforts via a more detailed course outline than normal. This will help you to get incremental buy-in and avoid making content changes in the development phase.

For the first course, the initial course outline and design document reviews went well; the writing style was accepted. We moved on to alpha development. But then, the stakeholder revised much of the content from a conversational to a formal 'voice.' – mostly so they could rewrite the course from the agreed-upon conversational language into more formal language.

> **Pause and reflect**
>
> Perhaps the stakeholder didn't adequately review the course outline or design document. Or perhaps another stakeholder that I wasn't aware of reviewed the alpha course and asked for the language change. It's hard to know.
>
> This company did not have a writing style guide or voice direction. In these cases, make sure you have ample examples of previous work to share the differences between conversational, professional, and formal writing tones, as well as examples of voice. Then, spend time asking them for their thoughts. Make sure you chunk alpha reviews into smaller parcels if you still think they need direction or may change their minds about the writing style used.

Lastly, later in the development phase, reviews stalled for several weeks as the stakeholder was traveling. To keep the project moving, other stakeholders were put onto the beta prototype review. Since they joined the project late in the game and lacked context, their reviews included alpha-level feedback and change requests at the beta level of development.

This is something that happens from time to time on ID projects. Stakeholders get busy and ask colleagues to fill in to complete their reviews, thinking they'll immediately grasp the project's context and approach the review as they would have.

Always provide and share a digital project timeline immediately and build in extra review time with a task-level line item for at least one additional reviewer – even if your stakeholders tell you otherwise.

> **Ask yourself**
>
> Overall, do you think a formalized kick-off presentation meeting could have helped this project?
>
> I do believe that some of the aforementioned delays would have still happened, regardless of holding or not holding a kick-off meeting. However, in retrospect, I think that *at least some* of these delays could have been curbed by investing in a formal kick-off deck, project brief, and digital project timeline **at the outset of the project**.
>
> Lessons learned!

This case illustrates a key point: you need to **provide structure** for your stakeholders – even if you think they're able to provide it on their own. Think ahead and create the structure *for* them, rather than assuming they'll get the process. You never know the knowledge level of a stakeholder – especially one that you have not worked with before. Bake structure into each project by creating a project brief, holding a formal kick-off meeting, and developing a detailed, shared project timeline at the very beginning of your project together.

You've now learned how agile communication and collaboration methods need to be put in place at the outset of an instructional design project and have read a use case that exemplifies this point.

Now, let's pivot to some handy resources to help you instill effective communication and collaboration on any ID project, throughout the ADDIE process.

Building your project communications competency

You are almost done with this chapter – and book! Congratulate yourself on the work you've done so far in reading about these four important ID competencies.

In this section, you'll find additional resources to help you learn more about agile project communication methods in instructional design. I've also included further resources surrounding communication and collaboration throughout the ADDIE process – including a few handy templates.

ADDIE versus SAM versus Agile

Some perceive the ADDIE model as slow and old, but with the agile communication tips we've discussed in this chapter, you can enhance your collaboration and embrace a more rapid and iterative design process – still using ADDIE.

Dig deep into this comprehensive article written by my former professor, Dr. Lisa Evans, that summarizes the various theories and models used in instructional design: `https://onlinedegrees.sandiego.edu/instructional-design-models/`. Toward the end of the article, there's a useful comparison of ADDIE versus the SAM frameworks of design and development.

In the preceding article, the authors call ADDIE a linear process. However, as we've discussed in this chapter, when ADDIE is approached with an agile communications mindset, it can transform into an iterative, life cycle-driven process – an eLearning project can be managed similarly to the SAM framework, but with more focus on the important implementation and evaluation phases.

Read this article to see how the kick-off meeting discussed in this chapter directly correlates with the concept of an agile savvy start meeting: `https://elearningindustry.com/addie-vs-sam-model-best-for-next-elearning-project`.

Finally, if you're wondering what the definition of agile program management is exactly, The Association for Program Management (UK) has this comprehensive definition:

> *"Agile project management is an iterative approach to delivering a project throughout its life cycle. Iterative or life cycles are composed of several iterations or incremental steps toward the completion of a project. Iterative approaches are frequently used in software development projects to promote velocity and adaptability since the benefit of iteration is that you can adjust as you go along rather than following a linear path."*

For more information on using an agile approach in PM, check out their website at `https://www.apm.org.uk/resources/find-a-resource/agile-project-management/`.

Making ADDIE more agile with project management tools

This section wouldn't be complete without a discussion of the digital project management tools you can use to guide your communication and collaboration throughout your project. There are many such PM tools on the market; you need not spend a lot of time or money choosing one. Even a tool that does not dig down to granular task-level assignments is more helpful than no collaboration tool at all.

I will say that I have a bias in this area toward the PM tool Asana™ (`https://asana.com/campaign/fac/do`), which I was introduced to when I worked on a learning project for a super-agile technology company. All team members and cross-functional collaborators used this tool, with each person fully owning their tasks.

We managed the design and development of eight courses from content analysis to evaluation – including a 12-person SME review cycle, numerous stakeholder and leader reviews, and even video and podcast development in *12 weeks* using this tool. I honestly don't think we could have accomplished what we did without it. I have a subscription that, at the time of this book's publishing, costs me $10.99 per month.

Another great PM tool is ClickUp™ (`https://clickup.com/`). I know many freelance IDs who use it as it offers a robust free plan, sharing capabilities, and different views such as lists, boards, or in Gantt style, similar to Asana™. Trello™ (`https://trello.com/`), is another tool that several of my freelance colleagues use. It also offers a free and a low-cost version at only $5 per month.

There are loads of PM tools out there. I found it helpful to experiment with a few using their free trial versions on a few actual projects before I settled on the one that I preferred most.

Kick-off meeting templates

I'd be remiss if I didn't provide a few files for the most important concept of this chapter: the kick-off meeting!

I've developed a few simple templates for you to download and use as you go to create your first visual project brief and plan for your next ID project's kick-off meeting. Please note that these are nothing fancy – just simplified templates that I've designed to help you get an idea of how to put what we've discussed in this chapter into practice. You can change them in any way that you feel suits your needs and organizational context:

- `Visual Project Brief.pptx: https://bit.ly/3zeCu9s`
- `Sample Project Kick-off Deck.pptx: https://bit.ly/40HisjH`

Working with stakeholders and clients

In the open source textbook *Design for Learning: Principles, Processes, and Praxis*, authors Lee Tran, Kathy Sindt, Rudy Rico, and Benjamin Kohntopp write about working with stakeholders and clients in *Chapter 34*. Much of what we've discussed is covered in this chapter, such as communicating the scope of work at the outset, setting up collaboration tools, and the review process.

However, the authors provide some additional files and templates for your use, as well as discuss ethical concerns such as plagiarism, which can be found at `https://edtechbooks.org/id/ working_with_stakeholders`.

Christy Tucker has several wonderful articles that discuss time estimates, project management, and working with stakeholders' expectations. This is especially helpful if you're trying to venture out on your own as a contract/freelance ID. Inevitably, your stakeholders *will* ask you how long it will take to complete a project! You can find this article at `https://www.christytuckerlearning. com/time-estimates-for-e-learning-development/`.

Christy's site also features a section that talks about getting started in instructional design. She has been featured on many podcasts:

- `https://www.christytuckerlearning.com/instructional-design- careers/`
- `https://www.christytuckerlearning.com/?s=podcast`

Feedback and course evaluation

There are many approaches we can take to evaluate the learning experiences we create. Authors Cheryl Calhoun, Shilpa Sahay, and Matthew Wilson present a thorough discussion of evaluation methods in instructional design in *Chapter 14* of *Design for Learning: Principles, Processes, and Praxis*. Evaluation methods such as Kirkpatrick's *Four Levels of Training Evaluation* and different approaches as to how and when we evaluate (`https://edtechbooks.org/id/instructional_design_evaluation`).

Often, course evaluation isn't often discussed at the outset of an instructional design project. This `eLearningindustry.com` article by Srividya Kumar highlights the need for *planning* for evaluation – and when and how to go about creating a course evaluation plan. She also offers an evaluation plan template that aligns with Kirkpatrick's Four Levels of Evaluation. (`https://elearningindustry.com/creating-elearning-evaluation-plan-ultimate-guide`).

Summary

I hope that this chapter on competency in project communications in instructional design has provided a thorough overview of how to manage communication and collaboration throughout the ADDIE process using agile communications methods.

Even if you haven't held a project kick-off meeting, used a digital program management tool, or managed an ID project – I believe by reading this chapter, you will now have the tools to implement effective communication and collaboration in your next project, whether it be with an external client or internal stakeholders.

You have now completed each ID competency chapter – *Teaching*, *Writing*, *Creating*, and *Communicating*. Thank you for reading this book and embracing the ID competency model!

In this book's *conclusion*, I've added some practical pointers for you to continue your ID competency-building journey. In the *Appendices*, you'll find downloadable links for the exercises mentioned thus far, as well as a few tools for your new *ID toolbox*.

6
The Next Level

"Self-belief does not necessarily ensure success, but self-disbelief assuredly spawns failure."

– Albert Bandura, social cognition researcher and professor of psychology

Whatever your reason for reading this book – whether you're trying to break into instructional design, or you're already doing ID work and need more direction – you're now familiar with The Four Competencies Model, and how improving your skills in each area will provide you with the capabilities needed for a successful career in instructional design.

I can... TEACH	I can... WRITE
I can... CREATE	I can... COMMUNICATE

Figure 6.1 – The Four Competencies Model

I hope that the concepts in this book have inspired you and helped you to:

- Identify your current skills and strengths
- Apply them to your career in instructional design
- Realize which areas you may need to build upon
- Develop your weaker competencies so that you become a well-rounded instructional designer who is capable of taking on all sorts of assignments.

By reading each chapter, you have probably identified your areas of strength – and other areas you may think you need to develop. In this concluding chapter, I'd like to discuss how to get you closer toward being that next-level instructional designer, starting with the concept of **self-efficacy**.

Self-efficacy and the Four ID Competencies

The late renowned social psychologist Albert Bandura (`https://albertbandura.com/albert-bandura-self-efficacy.html`) developed the concept of self-efficacy in his research, which he described as:

> *"Self-efficacy is the belief in yourself, and your ability to execute the necessary behaviors to attain performance in specific things."*

> *-Albert Bandura*

Self-efficacy is *your* belief in *your* abilities as related to dealing with various situations. These situations can be old, new, easy, or difficult. It can impact not only how you feel about yourself, but also how successful you might be at a given endeavor. A high level of self-efficacy has been linked to protecting ourselves against psychological stress, and even to a greater innovation. This interesting research can be found at can be found at `https://bit.ly/3ZSpamD`.

In the *Appendices* section of this book, *Appendix 6* and *7* are helpful tools for both gauging and improving your self-efficacy. We can think of instilling the Four Competencies as **a model for self-efficacy for instructional designers**. This book is about you realizing where you may sit on the continuum of each area and trying to move that arrow further along to the right. In turn, this will help you to *believe more in yourself* and to reach specific performance goals in your work and career.

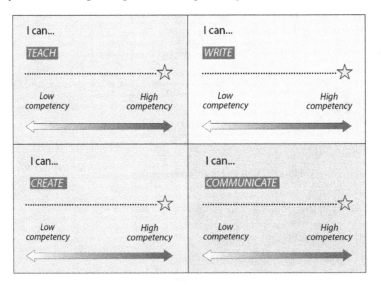

Figure 6.2 – The Four Competencies Model as a continuum of career growth

In other words, by acting on the information presented in this book, you are shifting from a "what I can do" *(task mentality) to a* "what I am capable of" *(high self-efficacy mentality)*. Building your ID competencies through high self-efficacy in your capabilities is more impactful and long-term than the ID task mentality. There are always new task-oriented tips and tricks that anyone can pick up, but these are not the essential key competencies of being an instructional designer.

Taking action

To gain self-efficacy, it's not enough to read, think, or talk about the Four ID Competencies; you need to take action even if it's only one small step at a time. You've already completed the first step by reading this book. If you haven't completed the exercises in the book, circle back and do them now. This is your next step toward your new-found belief in yourself and your competency as an instructional designer. Taking these micro steps will allow you to practice and start *believing in yourself* and your competency as an instructional designer.

Perhaps thinking about trying out some of the concepts in this book might make you feel uncomfortable at first. You can start by experimenting in small ways that will allow you to experience micro successes to build your belief and self-efficacy in your capabilities. Ultimately, it's your choice to accept the (possible) discomfort ahead and to choose to try these new concepts to grow your career.

To start building your self-efficacy and ID competencies, ask yourself the following questions:

- Are you willing to start building your weaker ID competencies by changing your behavior?

- What are you prepared to do right now?

- What action or small experiments can you take today toward instilling/building these capabilities?

Start by practicing. Set micro step goals toward building one competency area a day or maybe all four areas within a week. For example, you could:

Competencies	Teaching	Writing	Creativity	Communicating
TRY:	Using Bloom's Taxonomy action verbs and learning levels to write your next round of learning objectives	Practicing using the AIDA copywriting model in your next video script	Mindfully choosing to conduct "experience experiments" to open your mind about new people, places, or things	Creating a visual project brief for your next ID project (see *Appendix 4*)

Competencies	Teaching	Writing	Creativity	Communicating
TRY:	Using the *Target Audience Analysis tool* (see *Appendix 1*)	Checking carefully for redundancies in your writing	Using the "I like, but I wish" IDEO creativity exercise mentioned in *Chapter 4*	Using the savvy start/project kick-off deck template (see *Appendix 5*)
TRY:	Digging deeper into ID learning models, such as ADDIE or SAM	Learning more about the tips and tricks of video scriptwriting	"Embracing ambiguity," as an IDEO designer would	Investigating digital project management tools (or a new one if you don't like the one you have)
TRY:	Reading more about conducting a needs assessment	Bookmarking (`https://writingcommons.org/`)	Instilling a growth mindset by learning the laws of UX design, such as Miller's and Fitt's	Writing a very specific alpha or beta review request email, using the verbiage provided in *Chapter 5*
TRY:	Taking a deep dive into learning how to set performance goals	Reviewing the videos mentioned at the end of *Chapter 3* to learn more about storytelling in ID writing	Furthering your growth mindset by learning more about learner accessibility and UDL	Creating an evaluation and iteration plan for your next learning project

Figure 6.3 – Taking action! Examples

These are just *some* ideas! There are so many concepts, resources, and tools in each of the Four Competency chapters; the choice is yours about where you'd like to start. Trying out some of the on-the-job competency-building skills with an easy project (and a supportive stakeholder group) works best. By embracing these small experiments in "friendly" projects, you'll be on your way toward continuous learning across the Four Competencies – and your belief in yourself.

You now know what's important to build your career in instructional design, and how to build the four key competencies that successful IDs share. Now, put your knowledge and self-awareness into action, and embrace your new or continuing career as a *Next-Level Instructional Designer*.

Acknowledgments

This book was only made possible by the collaboration of the many people who provided suggestions, edits, and most importantly, their time and support.

To my technical reviewers, Robin Wagner, Jo Davey, and Scott Onstott – who not only reviewed the book on time but also provided many valuable opinions on how to improve this text.

To my editor Abhishek Jadhav, whose wisdom, practicality, and editing "eagle eyes" I am grateful for. Thank you for your support in this process!

To the rest of the Packt Publishing team, namely Himani Dewan and Amit Lockhande – who sought me out in the first place – and Manthan Patel, who endured my crazy schedule and was always gracious with requests for timeline extensions.

Lastly, a large thank you to the incredible instructional design program faculty at California State University, Fullerton – Cynthia Gautreau, Lindsay O'Neill, Sangeetha Carmona, and Lisa Evans. There would be no book if I had not completed this degree that enabled me to change my career trajectory – and life.

Appendices

Appendix 1

Target audience analysis

Objective of this resource: A quick at-a-glance guide to help you easily define your target learner audience. (**Sample Audience analysis**: `https://bit.ly/3LXi240`)

At-a-glance target audience analysis

Learner Demographics

What is your learner's:
- Age
- Gender
- Job
- Job expertise
- Job level (e.g., manager, leadership, employee)
- Primary language
- Formal education level
- Location

Knowledge and Application

- Does the learner have prior knowledge of this topic? Does it vary across learners?
- Is prerequisite/primer content needed?
- What are their professional goals?
- What do they need to learn?
- How much do they need this training?
- Are their hard deadlines for training the target learners?
- How will they apply what they learn on the job?

Learner Attitudes

- How much does your learner want to take this training?
- Do they think it will help them?
- What do you need to provide (statistics, research, etc.) to 'sell' the learner?

Learner Preferences

- How do learners want to learn - e.g., in-person, job aids, VILT, eLearning?
- What motivates them to learn - e.g., gamifiying, certificates, etc.?
- Do your learners like technology?

Audience analysis

Appendix 2

The ID writing assessment – source file and answers

Objective of this resource: Gauge your writing skills to see where your ID writing may fall short (also found in *Chapter 3, The Writing Competency*). The answers to the assessment are in the following section. (**Sample ID writing assessment**: `https://bit.ly/3Kb7rSm`).

Answers to Activity 1 – measurable learning objectives (LO)

1. Learners will hear lectures and attend discussions on future trends in medicine. (Yes / No)

    The answer is **No**. The LO could benefit from revision.

    A better LO statement may be:

    Learners will review five lectures and participate in five related discussions to recognize future trends in medicine.

    Why? Because *hear* and *attend* aren't really measurable verbs. Moreover, the number of lectures and discussions should be quantified.

2. Learners will select examples of the concept of a growth mindset from a list of examples and non-examples. (Yes / No)

    The answer is **No**. The LO needs revision.

    A better LO statement is:

    Learners will be able to identify the concept of a growth mindset from a list of examples.

    Why? Because *select* is not a measurable outcome verb. However, *identify* is. *A list of examples* is more concise language than *a list of examples and non-examples*.

3. Learners will understand the steps necessary for applying for a job. (Yes / No)

    The answer is **No**. The LO needs revision.

    A better LO statement may be:

    Learners will be able to describe the steps necessary for applying for a job.

    Why? Because, again, we need a measurable verb. A common mistake is to use *understand* instead of a more actionable Level One Bloom's Taxonomy verb. The learning objective becomes more measurable when *understand* is replaced with *describe*.

4. Learners will administer an allergy injection. (Yes / No)

    Once again, changes can be made. The answer is **No**.

    A better LO statement is:

    Learners will be able to execute an allergy injection successfully.

    Why? Because *administer* is not the most measurable verb. Using *execute* makes the learning objective more measurable. Furthermore, there are many wrong ways to give an injection; the LO's verbiage needs to point to the *right way* of doing it.

5. Learners will compute the mean, range, and standard deviation of a series of ten numbers. (Yes / No)

    The answer is **Yes**. This LO is concise, clear, and measurable!

6. Learners will have acquired the ability to deal with conflict. (Yes / No)

    The answer is **No**. The LO needs revision.

    A better LO statement is:

    Learners will be able to demonstrate the ability to deal with conflict by using the CARE strategy of conflict resolution.

    Why? Because this LO needs to be reworded into the active tense for clarity. *Acquiring the ability* is not measurable; better to use *demonstrate*. Lastly, there are loads of strategies to deal with conflict! Specifying which strategy is being taught yields a more concise LO.

Answers to Activity 2 – passive versus active voice

Each of the passive-voice sentences below has been reworded into **the preferred active voice**:

- **Passive**: The book is being read by most of the class.

  Active: *Most of the class is reading the book.*

- **Passive**: By then, the soundtrack will be completely remixed by the sound engineers.

  Active: *By then, the sound engineers will have completely remixed the soundtrack.*

- **Passive**: The user interface can be accessed from the desktop.

  Active: *The user interface is accessible from the desktop.*

- **Passive**: If you have questions, I can be reached at 555 555-5555.

  Active: *You may reach me at 555-555-5555 with any questions.*

- **Passive**: A path of destruction was left by the twister.

  Active: *The twister left a path of destruction.*

- **Passive**: Menu items can be added to existing OneClick menus.

  Active: *You can add menu items to existing OneClick menus.*

- **Passive**: The entrance exam was failed by one-third of the applicants.

  Active: *One-third of the applicants failed the entrance exam.*

Answers to Activity 3 – redundant writing

1. There is a possibility that the backup may not be successful.

   Rewrite: The backup may not be successful.

   'Possibility' and 'may not' mean the same thing.

2. Security must be increased to prevent violations.

   Rewrite: Increased security will prevent violations.

   'Must be' is unnecessary here.

3. The end result is exactly the same.

   Rewrite: The result is the same.

   A 'result' is inherently 'the end.'

4. The majority of applications ran smoothly, taking into consideration the high risk.

   Rewrite: Considering the high risk, the majority of applications ran smoothly.

   'Taking into' does not need to precede consideration.

5. With better advance planning, we can improve our current status.

   Rewrite: With better planning, we can improve our status.

   'Advance' and 'planning' mean the same thing in this context.

6. Results recorded over a period of time showed that CD-ROM discs were not suitable for this purpose.

   Rewrite: Results over time showed that CD-ROM discs were not suitable for this purpose.

   A 'period' means the same thing as 'over time.'

Answers to Activity 4 – typos and spelling

I've included the rewritten paragraph in italics, with a brief explanation for each error:

Original paragraph:

If you think about it, their is alot of data transferring on the sever. Because we do not have enough hard disk space, the only solution is to simply the amount of data that users need to excess. We will provides the documentation for this training, rather then having it done internally. There for, we must setup some log ins for its employees. We will need to altar some of the privileges so that vitally information does not leek.

Rewritten paragraph:

If you think about it, **there** (*there versus their*) is **a lot** (*two words*) of data transferring on the **server** (*misspelling from 'sever'*). Because we do not have enough hard disk space, the only solution is to **simplify** (*verb versus adverb 'simply'*) the amount of data that users need to **access** ('*to get' versus too much of 'excess'*). We will **provide** (*singular versus plural verb agreement*) the documentation for this training, rather **than** (*comparison versus sequence of actions 'then'*) having it done internally. **Therefore** (*misspelled*), we must set up **logins** (*one word or hyphenated versus two words*) for its employees. We will need to **alter** (*verb 'to change' versus religious 'altar'*) some of the privileges so that **vital** (*adjective versus adverb 'vitally'*) information does not **leak** (*verb versus vegetable 'leek'*).

Appendix 3

Mapping a learner's journey

Objective of this resource: To dig even deeper into your target audience's learning experience, create a design thinking-inspired journey map. You can do this on your own, with a group of people, or even virtually using tools such as Miro or Google Jamboard. (**Sample Journey map exercise**: `https://bit.ly/3Kdp3ge`)

Journey maps help us to think systematically about our learners and how they interact with the learning experiences that we create. Thinking broadly about their full learning journeys allows us to identify more opportunities for improvement in the process.

1. Choose the journey you'd like to map. In ID, it will most likely be the entire learning journey.

2. Before you create a visualization, write down the steps. Remember to include all the tiny steps the learner will be taking to understand all nuances that might ordinarily be overlooked.

3. Now, organize these steps into a visual map/timeline. You can branch your map to show options or keep it simple based on the steps you've identified.

4. Identify patterns that emerge, anything unexpected, and why certain steps happen in the order that they do. What insights do you glean from this analysis? How might you change the process?

5. Share your journey map with stakeholders who are familiar with the learning journey and ask them for their feedback to see whether you may have forgotten something or have steps that seem out of sequence.

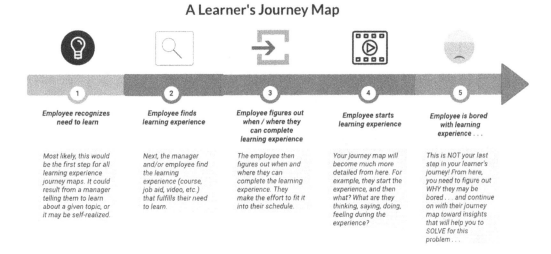

A learner's journey map

Appendix 4

The ID project brief

Objective of this resource: To identify what the general scope of work is for a given ID project in a visually engaging, at-a-glance format (also found in *Chapter 5, Project Communication in Instructional Design*). (**Sample Project brief**: `https://bit.ly/3z9HZ9B`)

How to give and receive feedback

Appendix 5

Project kick-off deck

Objective of this resource: A template designed for you to customize for your own *savvy start* deck to use during your project kick-off meeting (also found in *Chapter 5, Project Communication in Instructional Design*).

Sample Project Kick-off Deck .pptx: `https://bit.ly/40mgB46`

Appendix 6

Check your self-efficacy

Objective of this resource: If you're still wondering about the difference between Bandura's theory of self-efficacy versus self-esteem and where you may lie on a self-efficacy scale, check out the new *General Self-Efficacy Scale* created by psychology professors Gilad Chen, Stan Gully, and Dov Eden found at `https://bit.ly/3J4dLt8`. This research-backed tool will enable you to measure your own level of self-efficacy.

Measuring Your Self-Efficacy.pdf: `https://bit.ly/3KnM4NX`

Appendix 7

Improve your self-efficacy

Objective of this resource: A quick visualization tool to empower you toward taking the steps necessary to build your self-efficacy and belief in your own ID capabilities. (**Sample tool to improve your self-efficacy**: `https://bit.ly/3ZrjNdo`)

Improving Your Self-Efficacy

"Self-efficacy is the belief in yourself, and your ability to execute the necessary behaviors to attain performance in specific things,"   *- Albert Bandura*

01

MASTERY EXPERIENCES

Practice, practice, practice! The best way to master a new skill or improve performance is to practice it. By practicing, we are teaching ourselves that we're capable of acquiring new skills.

VICARIOUS EXPERIENCES

Watching others do something informs our own abilities. Positive role models, such as managers, colleagues, thought leaders, or friends and family members help us to absorb and emulate their healthy levels of self-efficacy.

02

03

VERBAL PERSUASION

Other people's words can have a positive effect on self-efficacy. Hearing that you are capable and can face any challenge ahead encourages and motivates. It also adds to one's growing belief in their own ability to succeed.

EMOTIONAL AND PSYCHOLOGICAL STATES

As Bandura stated, "Paying attention to your own mental state and emotional wellbeing is a vital piece of the self-efficacy puzzle." It's hard to have a healthy level of self-efficacy if you're not feeling emotionally or physically well.

04

05

IMAGINAL EXPERIENCES

Visualization exercises that allow you to imagine your future success in detail will help you to build the belief that succeeding is indeed possible. Visualizing attaining success can help you to feel more capable and empowered.

Improving your self-efficacy

Index

Packt.com

Subscribe to our online digital library for full access to over 7,000 books and videos, as well as industry leading tools to help you plan your personal development and advance your career. For more information, please visit our website.

Why subscribe?

- Spend less time learning and more time coding with practical eBooks and Videos from over 4,000 industry professionals

- Improve your learning with Skill Plans built especially for you

- Get a free eBook or video every month

- Fully searchable for easy access to vital information

- Copy and paste, print, and bookmark content

Did you know that Packt offers eBook versions of every book published, with PDF and ePub files available? You can upgrade to the eBook version at packt.com and as a print book customer, you are entitled to a discount on the eBook copy. Get in touch with us at customercare@packtpub.com for more details.

At www.packt.com, you can also read a collection of free technical articles, sign up for a range of free newsletters, and receive exclusive discounts and offers on Packt books and eBooks.

Other Books You May Enjoy

If you enjoyed this book, you may be interested in these other books by Packt:

Moodle 4 E-Learning Course Development

Susan Smith Nash

ISBN: 978-1-80107-903-7

- Build courses that emphasize the achievement of learning objectives.
- Write a variety of effective quizzes that can be taken online and offline.
- Make the most of the navigation and user experience improvements made to Moodle 4.0
- Encourage student engagement and collaboration.
- Incorporate functionality builders for more responsive and adaptive learning.

Canvas LMS Course Design.

Ryan John

ISBN: 978-1-80056-851-8

- Understand online learning as a powerful and unique tool for student growth.
- Create, access, and personalize your user account and profile settings in Canvas.
- Generate, upload, and import course content for students to engage with as participants in your courses.
- Discover expert techniques for designing a curriculum and creating activities.
- Explore Canvas features that meet your educational needs, such as online assessments and content delivery.

Packt is searching for authors like you

If you're interested in becoming an author for Packt, please visit `authors.packtpub.com` and apply today. We have worked with thousands of developers and tech professionals, just like you, to help them share their insight with the global tech community. You can make a general application, apply for a specific hot topic that we are recruiting an author for, or submit your own idea.

Share Your Thoughts

Now you've finished *Next-Level Instructional Design*, we'd love to hear your thoughts! Scan the QR code below to go straight to the Amazon review page for this book and share your feedback or leave a review on the site that you purchased it from.

`https://www.amazon.in/review/create-review/error?asin=1801819513`

Your review is important to us and the tech community and will help us make sure we're delivering excellent quality content.

Download a free PDF copy of this book

Thanks for purchasing this book!

Do you like to read on the go but are unable to carry your print books everywhere? Is your eBook purchase not compatible with the device of your choice?

Don't worry, now with every Packt book you get a DRM-free PDF version of that book at no cost.

Read anywhere, any place, on any device. Search, copy, and paste code from your favorite technical books directly into your application.

The perks don't stop there, you can get exclusive access to discounts, newsletters, and great free content in your inbox daily

Follow these simple steps to get the benefits:

1. Scan the QR code or visit the link below

https://packt.link/free-ebook/9781801819510

2. Submit your proof of purchase
3. That's it! We'll send your free PDF and other benefits to your email directly

www.ingramcontent.com/pod-product-compliance
Lightning Source LLC
Chambersburg PA
CBHW060155060326
40690CB00018B/4117